The Bike Bag Book

A MANUAL FOR
EMERGENCY ROADSIDE
BICYCLE REPAIR

A MANUAL FOR EMERGENCY ROADSIDE BICYCLE REPAIR

The Bike Bag Book

Tom Cuthbertson

ILLUSTRATED BY

Rick Morrall

TEN SPEED PRESS

1☉

TEN SPEED PRESS
P.O. Box 7123
Berkeley, California 94707

You may order single copies prepaid directly from the
publisher for $2.95 + $.50 for postage and handling.
(California residents add 6% state sales tax;
Bay Area residents add 6½%.)

Library of Congress Catalog Number: 81-50252
ISBN: 0-89815-039-6

Book and Cover Design by Beverly Anderson

10   9   8   7   6

Printed in the United States of America

THANKS

>to these among many others
who have helped along the
road: Julian Moll, Bryan Loehr,
Billy Menchine, Jim Rolens,
Dan Nall, Allan Neymark,
Laurance Malone and
Dan Steiling.

DEDICATED TO

>the jolly fellow (I never
caught his name) who gave so
freely of his time, tools and
parts, on that day when I
broke down out in front
of his garage in Dunsmuir,
California.

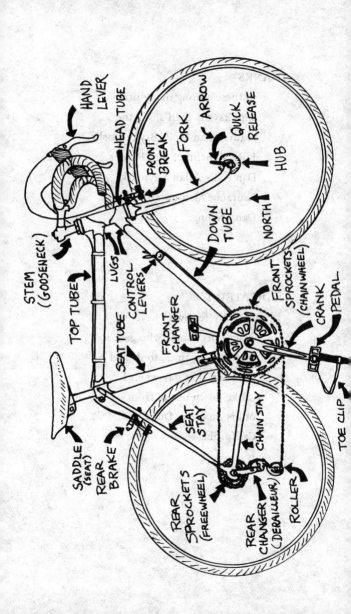

INTRODUCTION

This little book is about fixing bikes while out on the road. When you go for a bicycle ride, take the book, a few tools, and your common sense, and you'll be prepared for almost any mishap, from a flat to flobby fenders.

The contents of this book have been pared down from the original *Anybody's Bike Book*. Because of the limited size, this book can't cover every repair for every bike. That's why you take your common sense along. In some cases you have to read whatever material comes closest to covering your problem, then scratch your head awhile, then work out your own roadside solution to get rolling again. When you get home, use your shop tools and parts, and a full-size repair manual to get the bicycle in perfect order. This book is just to help you make it home in one piece.

When you do make it, using your own wits and muscles and limited mechanical resources, you'll get this great feeling of self-sufficiency. Boy, that's a fine feeling, and one that's getting all too rare these days. Read on, ride on, and enjoy.

Contents

1
Getting Set to Ride

To limit your troubles on the road, learn a few Rules-of-Thumb about the bike, ride at a time and place that make sense, and check your bike and road tools before you leave. That's simple advice, but the type we all forget. So here's a short collection of reminders.

Rules of Thumb

1. In this book, "left side" means the left side of the bike when you are sitting on it facing forward. The same goes for "right side."

2. On most bolts, nuts, and other threaded parts, *clockwise*, (often abbreviated *cl*) tightens, *counter-clockwise* (*c-cl*) loosens. Exceptions: left pedals, and some left-side bottom bracket parts. They have left-hand threads, bless their twisted souls; tighten them *c-cl*, loosen *cl*. Got it? Good.

3. All threaded parts are easy to strip. Before putting any two together, make sure they are the same size and thread type; start screwing one into the other BY HAND, slowly. If they resist each other, don't force their relationship. Back off. Get the parts to groove before you use any tools on them. And use only small tools, gently, to tighten small bolts and nuts. Tightening those 8 and 9 mm nuts takes deft pinkies, not beefy biceps.

4. Nine-tenths of the work you do to solve any bike problem goes into finding out just where the problem is. Even if you know what's wrong in a general way, don't start dismantling until you know exactly what is amiss.

You, your bike, and this book should go through the Diagnosis section on your problem one step at a time. Don't work on the bike without looking at the book, and don't read through a whole chapter of the book without looking at your bike. That way no parts will feel left out at the end.

5. Dismantle as little as possible to do any repair. When you have to take something apart, do so slowly, laying the parts out in a row, in the order they came off, on a clean rag or piece of paper or something. The more time you spend learning about the order of a unit's parts as you dismantle it, the less time it'll take to find the parts and put the thing back together.

6. Think twice before attacking rust-frozen parts. Is there any way you can get home without undoing them? If so, do it. You're liable to break them as you try to loosen them up, and chances are, you won't have replacements with you.

7. There are lots of ball bearings on a bicycle. Most spend their time racing around in happy circles between *cones* and *cups*. Either the cone or the cup of each bearing unit is usually threaded, so you can adjust how much room the balls have to play in. You don't want too much play; just enough to let the balls roll smoothly. To adjust any bearing set, first loosen (c-cl, usually) the locknut or lockring that holds the whole unit in place, then tighten (usually cl) the threaded part that's easiest to get at until you feel it squeeze the ball bearings. Then back it off (c-cl) a bit, usually less than a quarter turn will do, and finally re-tighten the locknut or ring (cl) so everything stays nicely adjusted. Spin the parts on its bearings. It should coast gradually to a stop. See if you can wiggle it

from side to side on the bearings. If it is free to wiggle more than a hair's breadth, or if it is not free to roll easily, readjust the thing. Keep those bearings oiled or greased, adjusted, and out of the rain, and they'll give you years of happy, free-rolling service.

8. Cultivate a fine ear so you can hear any little complaint your bike makes, like grindy bearings, or a kerchunking chain, or the slight creak-squeaking of a crank that is coming loose. You don't have to talk to your bike when you ride it — just listen to it affectionately, and take care of its complaints before they become big problems miles away from home.

9. Find a good bike shop in any area you are riding through, *before* you go through there, if possible. The good shops are not necessarily the big flashy ones; they are the ones with people who *care*. Do as much of your bike shopping as you can at these shops that care.

10. Don't be afraid to ask people out in the country if you can use their monkey wrenches or screwdrivers for repair. Use discretion about strangers if riding alone, but if you are in a group, don't be too shy. You'll be amazed at how many friendly folks there still are out there in the country. And in towns and cities, too!

When and Where to Ride

A quiet residential or country road on a sunny spring morning will make for a better ride than a six-lane city arterial during Friday rush hour.

Pick rides that make sense; it's as simple as that. Some hints that will help: avoid commercial streets by riding parallel backstreets; don't ride at times when drunk drivers are likely, such as Friday or Saturday night, or on warm holiday afternoons. Stay off routes used by heavy, pavement-bruising trucks if you can, and keep night riding to a minimum. The fewer hassles you have with traffic, potholes, and limited visibility, the fewer hassles you'll have with your bike. To keep damage to your head at a minimum, wear a helmet whenever you're going to be riding around cars, trucks, or dangerous road conditions.

Quick Maintenance Check

When you're ready to go on a ride, you don't want to spend much time fooling with your bike. But take a look at these few items and you can cover 95% of the trouble people have on the road.

1. Chain: Make sure it has a light film of 10-20 weight motor oil or bicycle oil on it. (See page 103.)

2. Tires: Make sure they're pumped up to the right pressure and that the tube isn't bulging out anywhere. (See page 58.)

3. Brakes: Just make sure they'll stop you. When you squeeze the levers, they shouldn't go more than half-way to the handlebars before the brakes are fully applied. Take a quick look at the cables, to make sure they aren't frayed (that is, some of the strands broken) at the places where they come out of the housing and attach to the lever and brake mechanism. Check the brake shoes to make sure they aren't loose or cockeyed. (See page 25.)

If you're setting out on a long ride, or a full day of touring, with a group, you may want to check a few other items to make sure you don't hold up the other cyclists with nagging little mishaps.

4. **Gears:** Make sure the little adjustable bolt holding the control lever is neither too tight nor too loose; you should be able to shift through the gears easily, and the changer should stay in whatever gear you put it in. (See page 112.) Then check to see that the changers can get the chain in and out of the lowest and highest gears without throwing the chain. (See page 111.) On a three-speed, check the indicator in middle gear. (See page 108.)

5. **Creeping Looseness:** Check the bolts, nuts, pins, or whatever that hold the following parts. If they show signs of looseness, see the indicated pages for more diagnosis and repair: Cranks (page 91, and make *sure* they're tight before taking off on a long trip); luggage carrier; Wheels (page 62); Seat (page 80); Handlebars and/or Stem (page 29); Headset (page 35).

Tools and Other Stuff to Take

You can't take every tool and part necessary for every imaginable repair, but for even fairly short rides take the mini-kit, and you'll be able to fix an amazing number of things if you will remember to use not only the tools but the gray matter inside your trusty helmet. That gray stuff can get you out of a lot of jams, even when you don't have the perfect tools along. Best of all, gray matter improves with use.

HELMET

GRAY MATTER

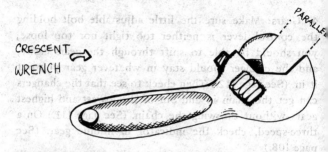

CRESCENT WRENCH →

PARALLEL

MINI-KIT

1. Crescent Wrench (adjustable end wrench). Get a good one. Attributes of a good one are a forged body, milled and hardened jaws, and a precise adjusting action. To test a wrench, open the adjustable jaw a little and see if you can wiggle it in such a way that it moves up and down in relation to the body of the tool. A good crescent wrench will wiggle very little, and the jaws will stay parallel. The six-inch size is best. Some people even saw the end of the handle off to make the thing smaller.

2. Screwdriver/Pocket Knife. A screwdriver with a forged steel shank and a thin blade end will be best. A pocket knife with a screwdriver will work fine, and it's good to have a knife for things like cutting your bread and cheese for lunch. Just don't do any heavy prying or tire-removing (see below) with your pocket knife or screwdriver blade. The screwdriver tip should be ¼ inch wide and the shank 4 or 5 inches long.

3. Tire Patch Kit and Tire Irons. The patch kit can be bought as a unit from any decent shop. It should have a tube of glue (keep the cap on tight or it'll dry out), several small and large patches (the kind that taper

out to thin, flexible edges are best), and something to scrape a rough spot on the tube, like rough sandpaper or a tin rasp. Cut out a ¾ inch by 3 inch piece of thin sidewall from an old tire and put it in there too. It will work OK as a "boot" to cover a slice in a tire in an emergency. Each tire iron should have a thin, smooth, rounded prying end, and a hook at the other end to fit onto the spokes. Make sure your irons are first quality; cheapo sharp-edged ones make holes in the tube like a screwdriver if you don't use them just right.

4. Spare Tire or Tube. If you use sew-up or tubular tires, carry at least one spare, and a needle and thread with your patch kit. For normal clincher tires, or "wire-ons" like most of us use, all you have to carry is a spare tube. You can put it in a little bag with the rest of your mini-kit and attach the bag under the rails of your seat.

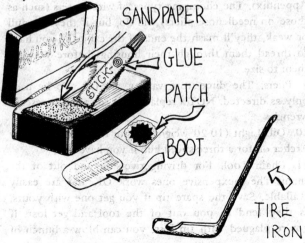

SANDPAPER

GLUE

PATCH

BOOT

TIRE IRON

5. Allen Key. 6 mm Campy "T" wrench or just a 6 mm L-shaped one, especially for lightweight ten-speed bikes.

6. Tire Pump. The kind that fits on a frame bracket, or between the top tube and bottom bracket of your frame. If possible get a *good* one that either pushes onto your tire valve directly or squeezes onto the valve with a thumblock mechanism.

7. Friend. No description needed. Take one on all long rides though, for parts-holding, morale-boosting, and, if things get really bad, help-fetching.

MAXI-KIT (for long country tours)

8. Cable cutters. The best is the heavy-duty bicycle cable clipper that grabs the cable in a diamond-shaped hole and shears it off clean. It'll cost you a bundle, but save you loads of trouble. Get one from a hot-shot bike dealer or order it from one of the bike catalogues (see Appendix). The chomping types of wire cutters (such as those on needlenose pliers) will do, but if they are dull or weak, they'll mash the ends of the cables so you have to thread them through their housings before you cut them to size.

9. Pliers. The dime-store variety are OK. To be used only as directed. NOT a replacement for a good crescent wrench.

10. Oil. Light (10-20 weight) oil for the chain, Sturmey Archer oil for a three-speed hub if you have one.

11. Chain Tool. For driving rivets in and out of the chain. The inexpensive ones work OK and are easily available. Save the spare tip if you get one with yours, as they tend to pop out of the tool and get lost. If you're plagued with tip loss, you can blow a bunch of

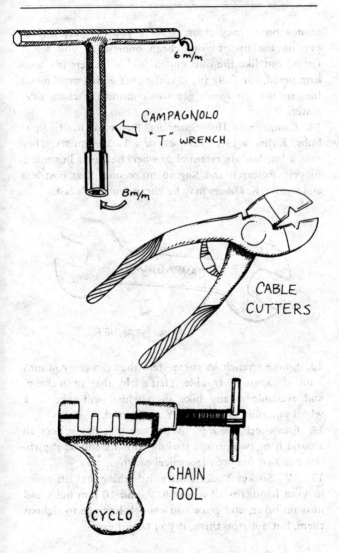

CAMPAGNOLO "T" WRENCH

6 m/m

8 m/m

CABLE CUTTERS

CHAIN TOOL

CYCLO

money on a fancy chain tool, or you can keep a close
eye on the tip of your cheap one; when you see it
flaring out like the butt end of a chisel where it's been
hammered, carefully file that flare off with a small metal
file, so the tip won't get stuck inside the chain side-
plates.

12. Campagnolo Hub Spanners. Buy two that fit your
hubs. Either a 13-14 mm set, or a 15-16 mm set. They
cost a lot, but are essential to wheel bearing adjustment.
Bicycle Research and Sugino make ones that cost less
and work OK. Others may be cheap, but don't last.

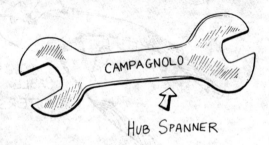

HUB SPANNER

13. Spoke wrench. A cheap item that can get you into
a lot of expensive trouble. That's why they're so cheap,
and available at any bike shop which will take on a
wheel you ruin. So use ONLY as directed.

14. Freewheel remover. A big nut that has splines all
around it or two prongs sticking out the end, as shown.
Get one that fits your freewheel *exactly*.

15. "Y" Socket Tool. A nifty little thing that fits easily
in your hand, fits all of the 8, 9, and 10 mm bolts and
nuts on bikes, and gives you enough leverage to tighten
them, but not strip them, if you take it easy.

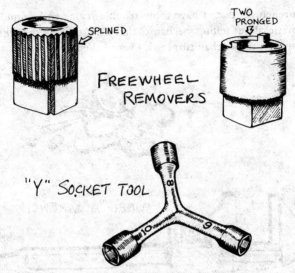

SPLINED

TWO PRONGED

FREEWHEEL REMOVERS

"Y" SOCKET TOOL

16. Spare Parts. Spokes (exactly the same size as the ones on your wheels, of course), a spare bungee cord or two, a couple of brake and gear cables.

ROADSIDE TOOLS

There are some things you don't have to lug around on your bike because you can pick them up almost anywhere. These include heavy sticks or two-by-fours that may be used to hammer things, stones that can be used as either hammers or anvils, and basic farm and car shop tools such as the Ford Model A or "monkey" wrench, the Channel Lock, the Vise Grip, and the Big Screwdriver. I have met farmers who chased me off their land, but I've never met a country mechanic who wouldn't let me into his shop to use a monkey wrench. In fact, I have more trouble trying to be diplomatic about telling mechanics that I'd rather fix the bike myself, rather than turning it over to them.

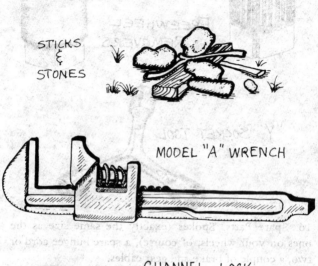

STICKS
&
STONES

MODEL "A" WRENCH

CHANNEL LOCK

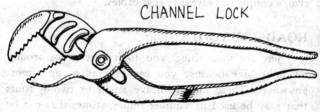

VISE GRIP

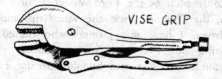

2
Brakes

GENERAL PROBLEMS: *Brakes don't go on*, or *Brakes don't go off*. Either you have no brakes, or your brakes work fine when you put them on, but then won't let go of your wheel. It's simple to say what those problems are, but often much harder to figure out just what in hell is causing the trouble.

DIAGNOSIS: *Brakes don't go on*. The problem is probably a loose or broken cable, or a whole brake system that is so rusty the parts are frozen together. See Cable PROBLEMS if it's just a cable bothering you. For a complete overhaul, see a complete manual and do the job at home, not on the road. Just ride home as slowly and carefully as you can, using your other brake.

Brakes don't go off. Something is sticking in your brake system so one or both of the brake shoes won't let go of the wheel rim when you let go of the brake handle. Any of the three units of the brake system, the Hand Lever, the Cable, or the Mechanism could be hung up. If your brakes get the "stickies" (a malady about as common to brakes as the common cold is to man), first find out which unit is stuck. Apply the brake. Move the hand lever back to its released position. If it moves freely, it's OK and you know the snag is in the cable and/or the mechanism. If the hand lever doesn't move freely, it has the stickies (see Hand Lever PROBLEMS). If the trouble is in the cable or mechanism, loosen (c-cl, and don't undo it, just loosen it a bit) the nut on the cable anchor bolt that holds the cable at its mechanism end. Don't pull the cable out of there! They're often a pain to get back in. Tug a little on the anchor bolt end of the brake cable with one hand and operate the hand lever with the other. When you release the lever, does the cable fail to slip back towards your tugging hand? If so, and the lever is OK, then you can bet the cable has the stickies. See Cable PROBLEMS.

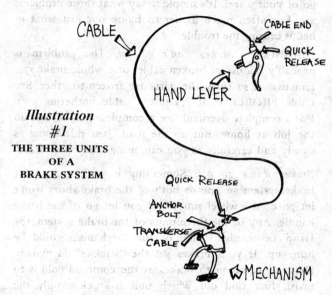

CABLE

CABLE END

QUICK RELEASE

HAND LEVER

Illustration #1
THE THREE UNITS OF A BRAKE SYSTEM

QUICK RELEASE

ANCHOR BOLT

TRANSVERSE CABLE

☞MECHANISM

Cable OK? That leaves the brake mechanism. Try squeezing and releasing it with your hand, reaching through the spokes with your fingers to do it. If one or both shoes don't spring away from the rim when you let go of them, or if one shoe is cockeyed, see Mechanism PROBLEMS.

Hand Lever

PROBLEMS: *Stickies.* On a ten-speed, the problem is usually a bent lever, due to dropping the bike or falling on it. See if the lever is twisted out of line. Compare it to the other one. Try to straighten it with your bare hands, holding the post in one and bending the lever with the other. Get it good enough to get you home. If it seems weak or still catchy and out of whack, make sure you replace it before your next ride. You don't want that brake to break the next time you really need it.

On three-speeds and some rare ten-speeds, a sticky lever can be caused by a tight adjustable bolt (see illustration 2). All you have to do is loosen (c-cl) the nut on that bolt, then loosen (c-cl) the bolt itself a half turn or less, then tighten (cl) the nut well and put a drop of oil into the works. It should perform like a champ.

If the *Whole Hand Lever is Loose,* so it slips around on the handlebars, you have to tighten the mounting bolt that holds it. On three-speed type hand levers (see illustration 2) this is a snap. Loosen (c-cl) the nut first, then tighten (cl) the bolt and tighten (cl) the nut as well, so it'll all stay put. On most ten-speeds, the mounting bolt is hidden down inside the post of the lever unit (see illustration 3). That makes it harder to tighten. Find and release the quick-release lever, if your brake system has one (see illustration 1). That'll give you a little slack in the cable so you can get your screwdriver (or on some rare bikes, a "Y" socket tool for the hex head) down into the post of the lever unit to tighten the mounting bolt. If your brakes don't have a quick release,

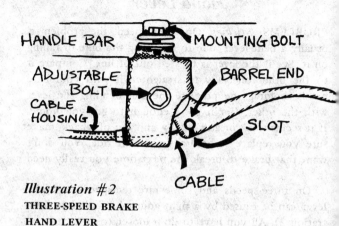

HANDLE BAR   MOUNTING BOLT

ADJUSTABLE BOLT   BARREL END

CABLE HOUSING

SLOT

CABLE

Illustration #2
**THREE-SPEED BRAKE
HAND LEVER**

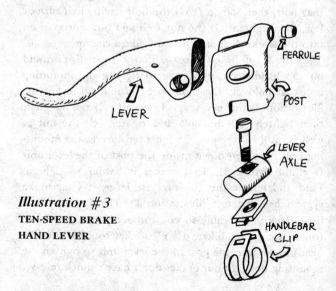

FERRULE

LEVER

POST

LEVER AXLE

Illustration #3
**TEN-SPEED BRAKE
HAND LEVER**

HANDLEBAR CLIP

have a friend squeeze the mechanism tight, or, if you can do it easily, remove the wheel and squeeze the brake mechanism all the way in to give you slack in the cable.

When the cable is slack and you have your screwdriver or socket in there to the mounting bolt, line up the brake lever the way it should be, even with the other one, and tighten (cl) the bolt firmly but *carefully*. If it strips or the head gets scrounged up, you'll never be able to fix it out on the road. Once the bolt is tight so the hand lever unit stays in place, tighten your brake by setting the quick-release lever, and you're ready to ride.

Brake Cables

PROBLEMS: *Brakes Loose.* You are screaming down the Italian Alps on your shiny new Cinelli and you see a hairpin curve coming up at you. Or you're cruising down to the corner market on your trusty-rusty three-speed and you see the grating of a storm drain that you never noticed before, about four feet in front of your front wheel. The bars of the grate, you notice, are wide enough for your wheel to fall between them. In order to avoid either the hairpin curve or the lethal drain grate, you slam on the brakes. Nothing happens for a terribly long instant. The next thing you realize is that the ground is coming up at you. Agh. Avoid this scenario. Keep the brakes adjusted.

Adjusting the Brakes means tightening the cable so you only have to squeeze the lever halfway to the handlebars to apply them fully.

If the brakes are just a bit loose (like, they stop you, but only gradually), see if you can find an adjusting sleeve for minor adjustments (see illustration 4) on your brake system. It'll probably be on or just above the brake mechanism. On some bikes, though, it'll be at the hand lever end of the cable, and it'll look a little different. When you find the adjusting sleeve, loosen (c-cl) the lockring and turn the sleeve up (*c-cl*, even though that may not seem right at first) to tighten the cable. Squeeze the brake mechanism with your free hand, so the brake shoes hit the rim, and you'll find it easier to turn the adjusting sleeve and tighten the loose cable. When the cable is tight enough, just tighten (cl) the lockring by hand, and you're ready to go. If you *can't* get the cable tight enough even by turning the sleeve all the way up, you have to do a major adjustment with the cable anchor bolt; turn the sleeve back down (cl) until it is at least halfway to its loosest setting, then tighten the lockring and go on to the next paragraph.

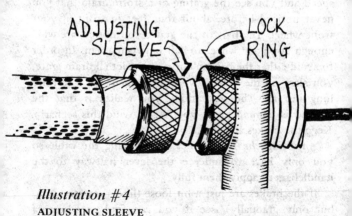

ADJUSTING SLEEVE   LOCK RING

Illustration #4
ADJUSTING SLEEVE

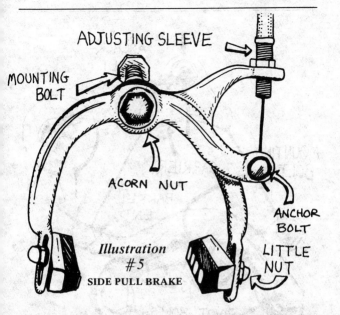

ADJUSTING SLEEVE

MOUNTING BOLT

ACORN NUT

ANCHOR BOLT

LITTLE NUT

Illustration #5
SIDE PULL BRAKE

A *Major Brake Adjustment* is hard to do on the road if you don't have two wrenches, or at least a wrench and a good pair of pliers, as well as a friend with strong hands to help you. Unless things are really bad, limp your way home cautiously, keeping your speed down and using your loose brakes early to stay out of trouble. In an emergency, though, you can get the brakes tighter. Find the anchor bolt and see if you can get a wrench other than the one in your mini-kit to fit it. Pliers will do if there's someone who can hold them tight and steady on the anchor bolt head while you use the crescent wrench on the nut.

Anchor bolt held still? Good. Now get the same friend who's holding it to use his or her other firm

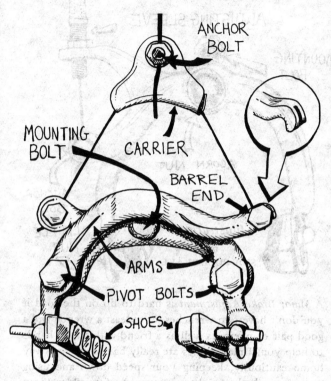

Illustration #6 CENTER PULL BRAKE

hand to squeeze the brake shoes in to the rim. When both the brake and the anchor bolt are held tight, loosen the nut on the anchor bolt, pull the cable tight (making sure it's as tight as it can be all the way along the line from the mechanism up to the hand lever), then tighten (cl) the nut on the anchor bolt firmly, until you can see that it has actually flattened out the cable in the little hole. This is hard to do with your friend's hands in there holding everything tight. The brake shoe gripping hand should be reaching through the spokes, so it's down below, out of the way. The hand holding the tool on the anchor bolt should be off to one side, so you can work on the other side. You should use both tools yourself and do the last hard tightening of the anchor bolt and nut. That way you won't twist the thing out of your friend's hand and mess up the bolt.

If you have to do this job on your own, good luck. Find a piece of string or wire or use a toe-clip strap to hold the brake shoes against the rim. That will leave both hands free to tighten the anchor bolt and nut. Don't expect to get the brakes really tight, though, and ride home slowly so the minimal braking power will still be safe.

If a *Cable is Broken*, the best thing to do is make sure the other brake is adjusted well enough to work, then ride home with extreme caution and replace the broken cable with a new one. If both cables are broken you have to figure out some way to use the rear one on your front brake.

First look at the end of the rear cable where it broke. Is the break near the mechanism end? If so, and if the break is a pretty clean one, all you have to do is take the cables out of their housings and put the rear one in the front brake system. Make sure you get the little ball or barrel at the end of the cable set firmly in its notch in the hand lever, then thread the cable through the little ferrules and the length of housing to the front brake mechanism. If the cable end is too frayed to go through the housing, you have to hunt around for a good sharp pair of diagonal cutters (called "dikes" by many mechanics) to clip off the frayed end. Some farm mechanics have them, most gas stations do, as do fire departments, utility and phone repairmen, and even some truck drivers.

Tighten your makeshift front brake as per the *Major Brake Adjustment* procedure on the preceding pages, then wind the extra cable up in a little coil and tie it that way, so you can ride home, slowly and cautiously. Do a complete re-cabling of both your brakes when you get home, using new, unfrayed cables.

Cables Sticky. If you ascertained, by the diagnostic method in the GENERAL PROBLEMS section for brakes, that your cable is sticking, it's probably because the thing is either rusty or kinked.

If the cable housing has a kink (a sharp, unnatural bend in the springy plastic covered tube the cable runs through), all you have to do is get a firm bare-hands grip on the housing on either side of the kink and straighten it. If the kink was at one end of the housing, like right above the hand lever, make a mental note to loosen and remove the cable when you get home, then snip off the bent end of the housing, thread the cable back in, and re-set the brakes. Don't try this on the road unless you have good clippers along. You may not be able to get the brake back together. Just straighten the kink as well as you can with your hands and ride home to your cable-cutting tool.

Brake Mechanism

DIAGNOSIS: Before you do anything to your brake mechanism, see if it is a side-pull type or a center-pull (illustrations 5 and 6). That way you'll know if I'm talking about your brakes in the instructions that follow.

PROBLEMS: *One-shoe drag.* One of the brake shoes refuses to get away from the rim of your wheel when you release the brakes. No matter which type of brake you have, loosen the nut that holds the whole mechanism to the frame of the bike. This nut will be on the opposite end of the mounting bolt from the mechanism. When it's loose, move the mechanism so the wheel rim is running right down the middle between the two brake shoes, then tighten up the nut with one hand while you use the other to hold the mechanism in that position.

Try the brake now. One shoe still dragging? On a center-pull brake this will mean something is really wrong with the mechanism, like a broken spring or a jammed brake arm. Limp home to fix those things.

If a side-pull brake drags one shoe persistently, though, it probably means one side of the brake spring is just pulling a bit too hard. You have to give it a whack to simmer it down. Get out your mini-kit screwdriver if it's a sturdy one, or find a big screwdriver or even just a big metal bar that's roughly the size and shape of a large screwdriver. Place the point of the screwdriver or whatever on the topmost point in the curve or loop of the brake spring, just to the side of the bolt where the shoe is *far away from the rim.* Not the side where the shoe is dragging.

Hold the screwdriver or bar as close to vertical as you can, and give the top of it a solid tap with a hammer or rock. Look at the shoes. If they are both off the rim, try the brakes and see if they both release as they should. It may take two or three taps to knock that spring down a bit. Don't hit too hard, though, or you'll knock the free shoe in until it drags; then you'll have to whack the other spring. Springs can take only so much whacking before they get too weak to do their job.

Stickies. If neither brake shoe comes off the rim when you release the handle, and the handle and cable are OK, the mechanism must be rusty, bent, or busted. Try some oil on the bolt or bolts around which the brake arms pivot. Squeeze and release the mechanism by hand to get the oil worked in there. Let it sit a couple of minutes while you go get a drink of water or something. Then try it with the hand lever again. Still sticky? Drat.

Squeeze and release the brake mechanism by hand again, watching to see if the brake arms are stuck on the bolt(s) or scraping against each other. That's usually the rub. Heh.

To free up a tight bolt, loosen (c-cl) it or the acorn nut and locknut on the end of it, squirt more oil in, and tighten up (cl) things again, locking the nut and locknut against each other so they're a bit less snug against the brake arms if you have side-pull brakes.

If the arms are bent or twisted so they scrape each other, try sticking a screwdriver between them where there's a bit of room, and prying, *gently*, until they bend just enough to free each other. If you have to bend anything more than an eighth of an inch, promise yourself to replace the brake mechanism when you get home.

Brake Shoe Cockeyed. You bumped your brake or it came loose, so one of the brake shoes hits the rim cross-wise or not at all. Fix it quick, before it wears a hole in the tire or gets launched in the spokes. All you have to do is loosen (c-cl) the little nut on the bolt that holds the shoe to the rest of the mechanism (if it isn't already loose), then move the brake around so you can see that it's lined up to squeeze exactly on the rim, then hold it there firmly with one hand while you tighten (cl) the little nut with the other hand. Take it easy on that nut. They strip out easily.

Brake Shoe Worn. If your brakes don't seem to work well and the shoes are worn down, first try simply tightening the cable (see *Brakes Loose* back a few pages). That should do it; brake shoes that are worn in to the shape of the rim can grab as well or better than most new brake shoes, as long as the whole system is tight. If you have trouble with your worn brake shoes slipping in wet weather or on wet roads, all you have to do is *think ahead* about your braking, then put on the brakes very lightly for a few seconds to whisk the water off both rim and brake shoes, so you can apply the brakes normally and come to a controlled stop, instead of having them slip and then grab in that terrifying way they can when they're wet. Another hint for better braking and longer brake shoe life is to use the brakes *intermittently* on long downhills so they don't heat up. If it's a steep hill, keep your speed down at all times by alternating use of front and rear brakes. Don't go all the way down a hill with the binders left on lightly all the way. That burns 'em up.

If your brakes are worn all the way down to the metal, see if there is some rubber left along the bottom edge. The shoe often gets worn more at the top, leaving a sort of ledge sticking underneath the edge of the rim. Take a pocket knife and cut the thinnest outer end of that ledge off. Then loosen (c-cl) the little nut on the bolt that holds the shoe to the mechanism and raise the shoe just a bit, so the new braking surface you've just made will hit the middle of the rim. Tighten (cl) the nut while holding the brake shoe in its new position, then try out the brake to see if you've got some stopping power. It won't be up to snuff, but it'll get you home if you take it easy. Get new brake shoes before your next ride.

Brake Shoes Squeaking. When you apply the brakes, your whole bike vibrates, and, if you're going fast, your brakes screech like a Model T with its original equipment. Don't let it bother you as long as the brakes stop you smoothly. If they are so juddery you can't make controlled stops, or if they're driving you NUTS on a long ride with lots of downhills, first check to see if the mechanism is bolted tight to the frame. Tighten (cl) the nut that's on the other end of the brake mounting bolt from the mechanism. Then see if either of the brake arms is hitting the bike frame. This is especially common on rear brakes. If it hits there, it'll screech and rattle.

To move the mechanism away from the frame, loosen (c-cl) and remove the nut you just tightened, then take

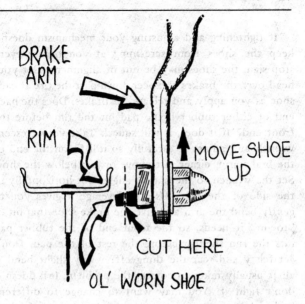

Illustration #7   **LAST DITCH BRAKE SHOE**

the washer from under that nut, and after removing the seating pads (washers with a curve on one side so they fit against the curve of the bike tube), put the washer next to the mechanism on the mounting bolt, then put the bolt through the seating pads and the frame so you can tighten it all up with that little extra bit of space you made by putting the washer in its new home. On some brakes this trick can't be done; you have to put up with the squeaks until you get home and replace the whole mechanism with one that misses your frame.

If tightening and adjusting your mechanism doesn't keep the shoes from screaming at you before every stop sign, the shoes may be out of alignment. Get your head over the brakes and peer down past the tire at each shoe as you apply and release the brakes. Does the back end of either rubber brake pad hit the rim before the front end? If it does, it will squeal. Take your crescent wrench and adjust it carefully so it'll fit on the end of the brake arm, either just above or just below the shoe. Set the wrench so the handle angles out horizontally to the side of the bike. Use the leverage it gives you to *gently* bend the arm and give the brake shoe that bit of "toe-in" it needs, so the front end of the rubber pad hits the rim slightly before the rest of the pad. Don't get feisty and tear the thing off; a very slight bend is all it usually takes to correct the problem. If it doesn't, don't fight it. You may want to change to different brake shoes when you get home, but I don't bother. As long as they work, I say, let 'em squeak once in a while.

3
Handlebars & Stem

DIAGNOSIS: For some reason, people often get confused about just what holds what in place on the handlebars and stem. If the handlebars swivel up and down (so when you lean on them your hands go down, or when you pull on them, they twist up and back) the *Binder Bolt is Loose.* If the bars are loose or if they aim off to one side or the other when your wheel is going straight, then the problem is a *Loose or Cockeyed Stem.* If your handlebars are too high or too low, this also requires working on the stem, not the headset, as you might suspect.

No matter what you're doing to either your handlebar or stem, make sure the ends of the bars are plugged. If they aren't, plug them immediately, before you get back on the bike and start riding. If you don't have official bar plugs with you, use a champagne cork or a wine bottle cork or even a short piece of stick with the end rounded off. Uncorked bars can be lethal in an accident.

PROBLEMS: *Binder Bolt Loose.* Tighten (cl) the nut on the end of the bolt that's under the stem. It's hard to get the thing really tight with a crescent wrench. You may have to get it just tight enough to hold OK, then ride to the nearest garage, bike shop, or friend's house to get a box end or socket wrench to really put the bind on the bugger. If the whole bolt spins around when you try to tighten the nut, the little key or "dog" under the head of the bolt must be sheared off; all you can do is

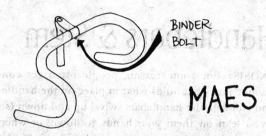

BINDER BOLT

MAES

ride to the nearest farm or garage with tools and borrow a pair of vise grips or strong pliers, then try to get a grip on the head of the bolt and tighten (cl) the nut as well as you can to get home. Then replace the bolt with a good strong one from a bike shop. If your bars slip because they are clearly too small in diameter for your stem, loosen (c-cl) the binderbolt nut all the way to the end of the bolt, then find a smooth, uncrumpled aluminum beercan (on many highways, they are all too easy to find) and cut out a 3 inch by 2½ inch strip of the side of the can with a sharp knife. Use this strip as a shim, wrapped around the middle portion of the bars where they fit inside the stem. Tighten up (cl) the nut as well as you can, and when you get home, tighten it extra-thoroughly with a box-end wrench.

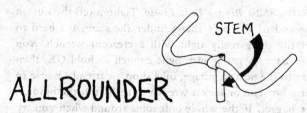

STEM

ALLROUNDER

Illustration #8   HANDLEBARS AND STEM

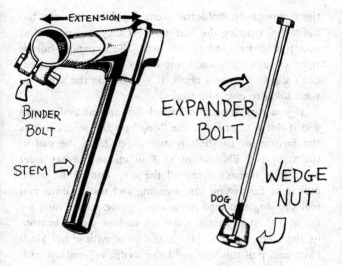

Illustration #9 STEM

Loose or Cockeyed Stem. To straighten bars that have gotten cockeyed, stand in front of the bike and hold the front wheel between your legs (don't get kinky with it, just hold it still). Grasp the handlebars firmly with both hands and straighten them so the stem extension lines up with the front wheel. If the bars won't budge, loosen (c-cl) the expander bolt, the head of which sticks out of the top of the stem (see illustration 9), then tap the head with a hammer, rock, or hardwood stick to unwedge the stem so it can be straightened.

Tighten (cl) the stem expander bolt if the stem is loose or if you loosened it to straighten the bars. Get it tight enough to hold the stem in place, but not too tight. Try twisting the bars again. If they stay put unless you pull quite hard to one side, the expander bolt is tight enough. It should not be so tight that the stem can't slip in case of a crash. If you fall on the bars, you want *them* to give, not you.

If you turn the expander bolt (cl) around and around and it doesn't get tight, the "dog" on the wedge nut at the bottom of the bolt is disengaged from the slot in the stem (see illustration 9). Pull up on the expander bolt. If it doesn't come all the way out of the stem, pull it as far as you can, twisting and testing until you feel the dog slip into its groove. Some wedge nuts are cut at a slant to match a slanted surface on the bottom of the stem, but the idea is the same with either kind; twist and pull the bolt until the wedge is lined up with the stem bottom. Then carefully hold the bolt up as far as it will go and at the same time twist it (cl) until the head snugs down against the top of the stem. Then use your crescent wrench or allen key to tighten (cl) the thing to the point where it'll stay put unless you crash.

If the expander bolt comes all the way out of the stem when you pull up on it, the wedge nut has come unscrewed completely. Try sticking the bolt back down there to get it started in the threads again. No luck? That's usually the case. Pull the stem out of the bike frame, then have a friend hold the bars and stem so the cables don't get snagged and kinked while you turn the frame upside down and shake the wedge nut out. Stuck in there? Agh. Such is often the case.

The best way to get the stuck wedge nut out is to remove the front wheel (see page 45), then take a screwdriver or piece of heavy wire or something, and poke up from the bottom of the fork tube to push the nut out. Don't use the expander bolt, or you might mess up the threads on it. And don't try to pry the nut out from the top; that may just get it wedged in there tighter.

When you get the nut out, turn it (cl) onto the expander bolt until it is settled into the slot or wedge shape at the bottom of the stem, then line up your brake cables so they are straight, put the stem back into the bike, get it straight, and tighten (cl) the expander bolt.

Stem Creaky or Cracked. When you ride up hills and pull hard on the handlebars, your stem creaks. It may be loose, or the wrong size, or cracked. Tighten (cl) the expander bolt as described in the previous section to make sure the stem isn't loose. Check for cracks on the stem, and look closely to see if it is the correct diameter so it just barely slips down into the fork column in the headset. If you see any sign of a crack on the stem, or if you think that it is too small in diameter, ride home gingerly, without pulling or leaning on the bars, and replace the stem. If a stem breaks or slips loose when you're really leaning on the bars, you take a fast and ugly fall onto the front wheel. Don't chance it.

Handlebars Too High or Low. On a long ride, especially if it's your first long ride on a ten-speed bike, you are almost sure to think, at some point, "My god, those bars are just *too* low for me. If I could just get 'em up a little, my back would feel better, I'm sure!"

Sorry. The bars are low for good reasons. Keep the top of them lower than the seat by an inch or so. This will lower your wind resistance so you can ride farther with less effort, and it'll put more of your weight on your arms, so your fanny doesn't take all the beating. If you feel like you're leaning forward too much, get home as best you can, then find out if you have the right size and shape bike. You might even want to use a sit-down type design, and stick to short rides. If you have a bike that fits OK, ride with your hands in a number of different positions on the bars, shifting from position to position every couple of minutes, so your back and neck don't get fatigued from the constant strain.

If you absolutely MUST change your handlebar height for some reason, the way to do it is to loosen (c-cl) the expander bolt about three or four full turns, then tap it with a hammer, rock, or hardwood stick. A stick or a 2 by 4 with a knot that you can bring down on the head of the bolt is fine. If you use something harder, you may want to protect the head of the bolt with a little sliver of wood or a popsicle stick or something, so it doesn't get scratched.

It doesn't take a real hard tap; just enough to loosen the wedge nut down in there. When the thing is loose, adjust the height of the bars, then get them straight, so the extension of the stem is lined up with the front wheel, and tighten (cl) the expander bolt enough so it'll hold the bars in place, but not so much that it can't slip loose in case of a crash.

4
Headset

DESCRIPTION: The Headset is the set of bearings that holds your front fork to the rest of the bike frame and allows the front wheel to steer. The fork tube or steering column goes up through the head tube of the frame, and all of those parts (see illustration 10) of the headset go around the fork tube. There may be some other parts on your set, such as a threaded washer instead of the one with the little tooth or "dog" on it, or a brake hanger or gear lever unit in place of that washer. Avoid taking all those parts out on the road if possible. Ride home and do the job in the peace and cleanliness of your garage or back room.

PROBLEMS: *Headset Loose.* The front of the bike clanks when you go over bumps. Or if you lift the front wheel off the ground and drop it a couple of inches, there is a clank. Or the fork seems loose in relation to the rest of the frame when you steer. Any of these common symptoms tell you the same thing. Either the front wheel is loose, or the headset is looser. Check the front wheel first. Let the bike sit normally on the ground and try to wiggle the front wheel from side to side with your fingers. If the wheel is loose on the hub, or if the whole thing is loose because the axle nuts aren't tight, see the Hub section on page 62. If the front wheel is firm, the looseness is in the headset.

　　To tighten it up, first loosen (c-cl) the big top lock-nut. If it's already loose, turn it with your hand. If it's tight, you have to find some kind of big monkey

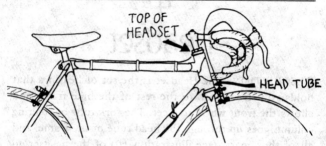

TOP OF
HEADSET

HEAD TUBE

wrench or channel lock pliers to get it loose. Most
farms, garages, and even gas stations have wrenches
that'll do the trick.

See if the washers or other parts between the top
locknut and the top threaded race are all loose now.
There may be a threaded washer still holding things
tight. It will have notches around it. Stick your screwdriver in one of these notches and tap the threaded
washer around (c-cl) a half turn or so to loosen it.

Now the top threaded race should be free to turn.
On some headsets, like the great Stronglight ones, there
are little teeth between the threaded race and the washer
above it. You have to loosen all the top washers and
stuff enough to pull that toothed washer up and dis-
engage it from the threaded race.

Tighten (cl) the threaded race down on the bearings
as far as you can by hand, then back it off a tiny bit,
so the fork can steer easily without jiggling around
at all on the bearings. Then lower or tighten (cl) all
the washers back down snug against the top threaded
race, then tighten (cl) the big locknut with the wrench
so it'll stay put.

If you're out in the middle of nowhere and the headset is loose, you can just tighten (cl) the threaded race

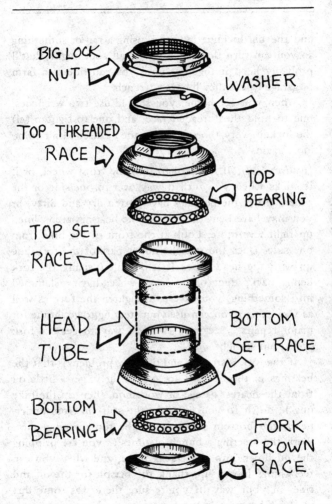

BIG LOCK NUT

WASHER

TOP THREADED RACE

TOP BEARING

TOP SET RACE

HEAD TUBE

BOTTOM SET RACE

BOTTOM BEARING

FORK CROWN RACE

Illustration #10
HEADSET, EXPLODED VIEW

and the big locknut by hand, using a rag or something so you can turn that locknut with all your might; that'll probably keep it together until you can ride to a farm or garage where they'll have a wrench.

When you get home, you should use two wrenches, one to hold the threaded race, and one to tighten (cl) the locknut very thoroughly, so the headset won't come loose again.

Headset Stiff. If it's hard to turn the front wheel, or if it sticks when you turn it way over to one side or the other, either the bearings have gotten dry and dirty, or you may have bent the fork so the bearings aren't lined up right any more. Look at the front of the bike from one side. Does the straight upper part of the fork line up with the head tube? If it doesn't (usually the fork bends back, due to the front wheel having slammed into something) you have to straighten the fork as well as you can so you can use your steering to get home for major repairs. See page 39 for a way to get the fork pulled out straight.

If the fork is straight and the only problem is that the bearings in the headset are dry or dirty, get a little oil from the nearest garage or workshop, then tip the bike upside down so you can drip the stuff in from underneath the bottom set race and the top threaded race. Work the steering a bunch of times as you are dripping the oil down into the cracks there, and when you can feel things loosen up, thank the person for the oil and ride on your way. If you're sure there was some dirt in those bearings, make a note to do a complete overhaul of the headset when you get home.

5
Frame & Fork

There's not much you can do on the road to fix things like a bent frame or a broken brazed joint. If you get a good bike frame and ride reasonably, though, the frame will probably never give you any trouble. The fork, on the other hand, may get knocked around some day.

PROBLEMS: *Fork Bent.* You hit something like a curb or a bad pothole or a big rock, and your front wheel is bent back so far that it almost hits the frame when you steer from side to side. If you can limp home on the bike the way it is, do so. If it is so bent you can't ride right, you can try the following trick. Cyclocrosser Dan Nall showed me how to do it when we were out in the deep woods with a guy who had "lunched out" in a creek bed.

Have a friend hold the bike up straight, or lean it against a post or a tree, and sit down on the ground with the front wheel resting between your thighs. I know it's a weird position, especially if your friend has a nasty sense of humor, but you want to fix the thing, right? Push the pedals around with your toes until they are straight up and down, then put the balls of your feet on the bottom bracket (where the axle for the cranks and pedals goes through the frame).

Now grab either the ends of the fork or the rim of the wheel where it is nearest to your chest. The taller you are, the easier it'll be to pull on the rim. If you're less than five feet tall you may have to take the front wheel off so you can pull on the drop-outs at the ends of the fork.

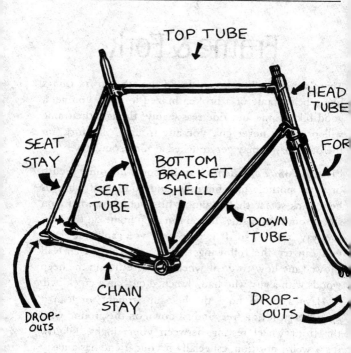

When you have a good grip on the rim or fork, straighten your back (you'll strain it if it's curved) and try to hold the fork or wheel absolutely still as you push the bottom bracket and the rest of the bike away from you with your feet. Make your legs do the work, not your back and arms. On many lightweight bikes, you will be amazed at how easily you can straighten those forks. On some kid's heavy-duty models, you won't be able to straighten them no matter how hard you push. Don't push so hard you bust a gut. You can try sitting two people down, one on each side of the bike, but even that may not work on a super-strong fork.

Whatever you do, don't leave a bent and straightened fork on the bike for good. When you have limped home, take the fork out of the headset, take it to a fine bike shop, and see if the thing can be accurately corrected by a pro frameworker, or if it should be replaced. And next time, keep a sharp eye out for those rocks, curbs, and potholes!

6
Wheels & Tires

DIAGNOSIS: When you're on the road, the most common wheel problem you'll have is a flat tire. Boy, are they common. If you get one on a racing tubular or "sew-up" tire, just switch the whole tire and ride home on your spare. When you get one on a standard "clincher" or "wire-on" tire, go to the *Flat* procedure just below and run through it step by step so you get the thing fixed correctly. If you don't have a flat, but your *Tire is Soft*, see the pump-up procedure on page 58.

If your wheel is loose or if it's making grindy-crackly noises, see Hub PROBLEMS on page 62. Don't ride with a loose or grindy hub, or you may ruin the bearings or even the whole wheel.

If your wheel is bent and wobbly, ride it home and either take it off and take it to a pro to be "trued" or do the job yourself when you've got lots of time and a good book or teacher to make sure you do more good than damage to those delicate spokes and rims. If you're stuck out on your own, though, and *have* to get the wheel closer to straight in order to get home, see *Bent Rim* on page 66.

Tires

PROBLEMS: *Flat.* Bah. You got a flat. Don't let it get you down. Cyclists have been dealing with them for a long time. Follow the procedure below, and you'll soon be on your happy way.

Flats are due to either slow leaks, quick leaks, or

blowouts. No matter what kind of a flat you have, *don't ride the bike on a flat tire! Not even on a soft tire!* The tire, the rim, and your very life are at stake. Even pushing the bike along on a flat may be bad for the tube valve. When you get a flat, carry the bike to the nearest place where you can stop and fix it. A shady spot under a tree is ideal.

Check the valve if you think it might be the cause. Pump up the tire. Spit or put a little water on your fingertip and put it lightly over the end of the valve. Tilt your finger tip a wee bit so the only thing between it and the valve end is the water (on a presta valve, like they have on fancy racing bikes, this will take two moist fingers). If little bubbles come through the water, your valve stem is loose. If you have a metal cap for your valve, like the one in illustration 11, you can stick the prongs of the cap down into the valve and loosen (c-cl) then tighten the stem down in there to see if this will stop the leak. Otherwise, you have to follow the wheel and tire removal and replacement steps in this section to take the tube out and put in your spare.

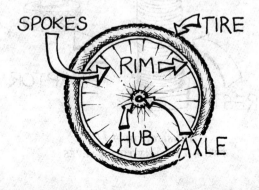

SPOKES   TIRE
RIM
HUB   AXLE

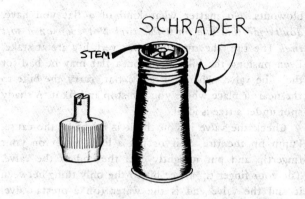

SCHRADER

STEM

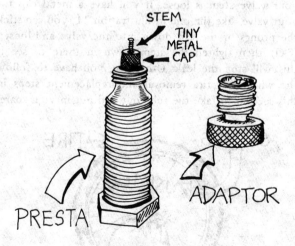

STEM
TINY
METAL
CAP

PRESTA

ADAPTOR

Illustration #11
TWO DIFFERENT TIRE VALVES

A good shop may be able to rescue your leaky valve stem, so don't throw the thing away in anger.

To patch or replace a popped or leaky tube there are a bunch of necessary steps. Hang the bike up, then remove the wheel, then get the tire off, deal with the tube, then put the tube back in the tire and get the tire back on the rim, and finally put the wheel back on the bike. It's gonna take some time. If you don't get harried, though, you can be back on the road in ten minutes, without causing any secondary problems as you fix the flat.

For a start, find something to hang the bike up on, like a fence post or a low tree limb. Even a sturdy bush or a patient friend will do. If you have bungee cords (the stretchy things with hooks on the ends), use one to hold the bike up so it can't fall down on you. It doesn't have to be held up high, just enough so the flat tire is a few inches off the ground.

Next thing to do is look at what's holding the wheel to the bike. There'll be big nuts on the threaded ends of the axle, or a little lever on the left side of the wheel, called a quick-release lever.

If you have a flat on a front wheel, all you have to do is loosen (c-cl) the nuts or pull the quick-release lever out, away from the center of the wheel, and the wheel will slip out of the front fork.

If you have a rear wheel flat (and they're much more common), don't loosen the nuts or the quick-release lever just yet. First get the bike in its highest gear. If the bike is a ten-speed, that means getting the chain onto the smallest sprocket in the back. If it's a three-speed, unscrew (c-cl) the adjusting sleeve (see illustration 30) all the way off the end of the indicator, then unscrew (c-cl) the indicator, pull it out of the hub, and screw the sleeve back onto its threads a bunch of turns so you don't drop the little thing in the dirt.

Now you can loosen (c-cl) the big axle nuts or the quick-release lever. When the wheel is free to move, squat or sit behind the bike, put your left hand on the rim of the wheel where it is nearest to you, and with your right hand grab the body of the rear gear changer or "derailleur" (on a three-speed you have to grab the chain between two fingers).

Push the wheel forward and down with your left hand as you pull the gear changer and chain back toward you. This action, with a little jiggling of the wheel, will get the rear sprocket free of the chain. Keep the jiggling to a minimum, to get the wheel out of there without tangling the chain up and pulling it off the front sprocket.

If the tire hangs up on the brakes, you can undo the brake quick-release lever if you have one (see illustration 1), or use the adjusting sleeve (illustration 4) to loosen up the tension on the cable.

Once you've got the wheel off the bike, you have to get the tire off one side of the rim. First push in the little stem tip on the valve (on presta valves, loosen, c-cl, the tiny cap before you push the stem tip in) and get all the remaining air out of the tire. Run your fingers all the way around the tire, squeezing and pinching the beads (edges) in to loosen them if they're stuck to the rim. This will give you an idea of how tough it's going to be to get the tire off the rim entirely. If it is quite loose, grab it with both hands in one place and pull away from the center of the wheel, so one bead or inner edge (see illustration 12) of the tire stretches up. Lift that stretched-up place over the rim, then work your way around the wheel, spreading the section of bead that has been pulled over the rim. This will be possible only if the tire is a loose-fitting one.

If the tire is a tight high-pressure one and you can't pull a section of the bead over the rim, use your tire irons. Do *NOT* use a screwdriver or any other substitute. Stick the round, spatula-shaped end of your tire iron a little way under one of the beads of the tire. Nudge the sidewall of the tire in with your fingers to make sure the iron doesn't grab on the tube, or go under both beads of the tire and pinch the tube between. Pinching the tube can easily put a hole in it, even if you are using tire irons. When you have the iron under just one bead of the tire, pry all the way out and down, then hook the handle end on a spoke (see illustration 12).

With a second iron, pry out more of the bead a couple of inches from your first pry. If you need to make a third pry and have only two irons, hold the bead outside the rim with your thumb, then pull that iron out, move it a couple of inches, and do another pry. Usually, though, two pries will get the tire bead well on its way.

When the bead is on its way (when it doesn't try to jump back onto the rim), take the tire irons out, stick one iron between the popped-out bead and the rim, and peel the rest of the bead out of the rim, just like you'd pare a giant potato peel. You've now got the

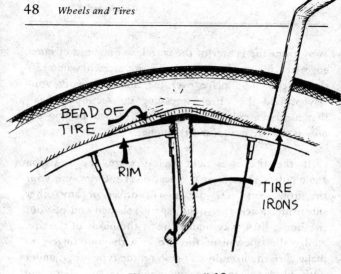

Illustration #12
USING TIRE IRONS

tire half off the rim; don't take it any farther off; that just makes more work putting it back on.

Pull the tube out of the tire, *except* where it is held by the valve. Leave the valve sticking through the rim and pump up the tube until it swells to about one and a half times its normal size. If the thing won't hold any air at all, the leak must be a really bad one, and easy to find. You'll probably have to simply replace the tube with your spare and hope you don't get any more flats on your way home.

If the tube does fill up, look for the leak. You may have to move your ear around the tube, listening for it, or even pass the tube close to your eye to feel the air against the delicate surface of your eyeball. Some pinpoint leaks are hard to spot. Don't wet the tube if you can avoid it; those bubbles from a leak are easy to spot, but the wet tube must be dried *completely* before patching.

When you do find the leak, mark it so you don't forget where it is. If you have a little pen or crayon in your patch kit, make arrows or "cross-hairs" pointing at the leak from about one inch away on each side. If you have no marker, use the sandpaper or metal scraper in your patch kit to "rough up" a 1-inch area of the tube, making sure your leak stays in the exact center of this rough area.

Figure out what kind of hole it is and what made it. Find out *now*, before you forget. There's nothing worse than getting two flats from the same cause. If the hole is a small round one, look for a nail, staple, tack, or thin shard of glass embedded in the tire casing. If you line the tube up with the tire, it's usually easy to find the culprit. If the hole is a small gash, there will probably be a bigger slash in the casing of the tire. If the slash is over ¼ inch long, you'll have to put a "boot" under it when you put the new or repaired tube back in. If the hole is on the inner side of the tube, look for a sharp spoke end poking through the rim strip. If there are two tiny holes on the inner curve of the tube (they're called "snake bites" in the trade), they are due to the rim and tire bead pinching the tube because it was under-inflated. You went over a sharp rock or pothole, and the shock of the blow made the tire bead chomp down on the tube.

Remove any puncture-causing debris you find stuck in the tire casing. Run your finger gently around the inside of the casing while you're at it. Might as well root

out any sources of further flats before they happen.
If the rim is rough (like at its joint) near the point where
you have snake bite punctures, use your sandpaper to
smooth out that roughness.

If there's a sharp spoke end sticking up, pull the rim
strip away from it, set your screwdriver tip on one side
of the spoke end, and tap the screwdriver with a rock
or something, so you can bend that nasty thing over.
If it's too short to bend over, file it as smooth as you
can with your sandpaper from your patch kit, then put
a little wad of rag or paper or a spare tube patch over
the thing, so it can't poke through the rim strip and into
the tube again. Make a mental note to take the spoke
out when you get home and replace it.

When you have found and removed or filed down the
cause of your tube leak, hold your finger over the hole
in the tube, pump the thing up again, and listen and
look your way around it once more, to make sure there
isn't a secondary leak hiding in the woodwork. When
you're sure you've found all the leaks and taken care of
what caused them, deflate the tube completely.

To get the valve out of the hole in the rim, first
unscrew (c-cl) any ring or nut that might be holding
the valve in there, then pull a six-inch section of the
tire bead *that you already took out of the rim* back
over the tube at the valve location. This will leave the
tube free to be pulled directly away from the center of
the wheel, thus slipping the valve straight out of its
hole in the rim.

If you have a spare tube that's in good shape, skip
the next few paragraphs and go on to the section on
how to replace the clincher tube and tire.

If you don't have a spare, or if your spare already has a leak, and you have a small hole, like 1/8 of an inch in diameter or less, you can patch it. Some bike shops refuse to patch any tube with a leak. They just put in new tubes. Haughtily they quote Webster, who states that a patch is a "temporary repair." They pronounce that in their shop, only permanent repairs are done. They have a pretty good point, but if you have only one spare and you get two punctures, you may not give a big damn about the temporary nature of the tire patch. What in the world *isn't* temporary, you might ask.

Clean and dry the tube around the hole, and rough up the surface with your scraper or piece of rough sandpaper if you haven't already done that. Make sure the hole stays at the center of the roughed up area, so you will put the glue in a circle with the hole in the center, and then stick the patch on with the hole in the center of it, too. The roughing and gluing often hide the hole, so it's best to have those arrows pointing to the hole from outside the scene of action.

Put the glue on quickly and lightly. Make a smooth, even, thin film of the stuff, larger in area than the patch, without any big blobs or dry places. If you do it right, it'll all look wet and shiny for a few seconds, and then it'll all turn a dull matte texture as it dries. Don't blow on it to make it dry quicker. If you spit or blow damp, misty breath on it, the patch won't stick as well.

If you've never done any patching before, you might want to practice the critical spreading of that thin patch of glue on some other part of the tube where there's no hole. Squeeze and spread a drop of the stuff out of

the tube and, if necessary, rub it very quickly and lightly
with a *clean* finger tip to make that smooth, even,
blobless film that will dry all at once and leave a con-
sistent matte surface for the patch to latch onto. Put
some dust over your trial glue area (so it won't stick to
the rim and tire), then go back to the roughed up
area around the hole and do the real thing, to per-
fection.

Wait a couple of minutes for the glue to dry completely. Make sure no water or dust gets on it. Then
take out the patch and see if it's small enough to fit
inside the glued area. If it's going to fit, take the little
oilcloth, tinfoil, or paper cover off the sticky side of
the patch, being careful to keep your fingers off the
sticky stuff as much as possible. If there's a thin piece
of cellophane on the non-sticky side of the patch, leave
it there so you have something to hold and something
to push against when the patch is in place. If there
isn't any neato cellophane on the patch, just hold the

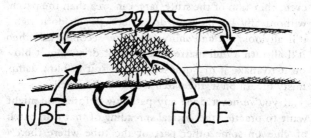

Illustration #13A   **PATCHING TUBE**

very edge of the thing with one fingernail while you peel the cover off the rest of the sticky side.

Stick the patch in place, making sure it lies down smoothly, without ripples or bumps. Then pinch and knead the patched tube between your fingers, starting at the center of the patch and working out to the edges. Squeeze it as hard as your fingers can, maybe stacking up the fingers of both hands to double your squeezing power. Make extra sure it's tight along the little lines or seams on the tube; those seams can make little channels for the air to seep out of if the patch isn't gripping really tight on them.

When you're sure the patch is on there to stay, and stuck well around all the edges, take a little fine dust or ashes or something and poof it around the patch, so the extra glue that's showing will get a light coating on it. That way it won't stick to the inside of the tire or the wheel.

Your patched tube is ready for use immediately.

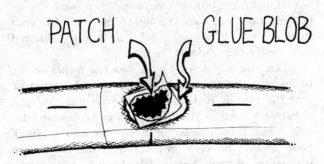

PATCH   GLUE BLOB

Illustration #13B   STICK THE PATCH IN PLACE

Pump the thing up, but not so much that it bulges out more than one and a half times its normal size. Run your eye and ear around the tube for a last check to make sure it doesn't have any more holes or a leaky stem.

To *replace the clincher tube and tire*, start by letting almost all the air out of the tube. If you are putting on a brand new tube, pump a bit of air into it so it isn't flat and unmanageable. If you are putting on a new tire too, get one of the beads around the rim, using your bare hands *only*. If you can't get that first bead on without irons, it's the wrong size. It might be hard to push the last inches of the bead over the rim, but puff and cuss and do it by hand.

You now have one tire bead in the rim and one bead free of it. Find the hole in the rim for the valve, and push the free bead of the tire at that point all the way over the rim until you can see the valve hole. Poke the valve in there, then pull the free bead back over the tube. Working away from the valve in both directions, stuff the tube up into the tire and tuck it into the rim, out of sight and out of your way. Then work the remaining tire bead over the lip of the rim with your thumbs, making sure the tube doesn't get pinched between the tire bead and the rim.

When you get down to the last few inches of the tire bead, it will get tough. Roll up your sleeves. Make sure the tube is tucked in out of your way, and just about completely deflated. If you can find some "dry lube," like baby powder or really fine dust or ashes, poof some of the stuff on that last bit of bead to help it slide over the rim. Even a dab of water or spit on the bead may help you get it on.

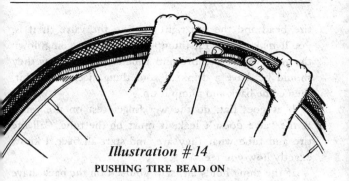

Illustration #14
PUSHING TIRE BEAD ON

Work with both thumbs on one section of the bead, as shown in illustration 14. Don't try to pop the whole thing over the rim at once until you only have a couple inches to go. It takes a lot of oomph on those thumbs, especially if you have a tight-fitting high-pressure tire. Just don't slam the wheel around in your excitement — they bend easily. And *don't* use a screwdriver, or, if you can possibly avoid it, even the tire iron. Anything you stick under the tire at this juncture could reach in there, snatch the tube, and pinch a hole in it.

Just get the bead on with those thumbs, a bit at a time. Franz Kafka once wrote, "There is only one human sin — impatience." Not that I expect you to keep your patience when the tire bead bites your finger, then jumps off the rim, allowing the tube to flap out at you like a kid sticking out his tongue. Just don't throw the wheel in your anger; they bend, remember.

When you finally get the bead onto the rim, go back to the valve and push it in and out of the rim a couple of times, wiggling the tire between your fingers as you do so, to make sure the tube isn't pinched between the tire bead and the rim right next to the valve. If it is, you'll make an awful thump-thump-thump going down the road. When the tire and tube are seated in as they should be, have a drink of something nice, relax a bit, then come back and pump it up.

If it goes flat, do the wet finger test on the valve. If the valve doesn't leak, it must be the tube. Call the tire and tube what they are, and start all over. I know exactly how you feel.

If the thing holds air, slap yourself on the back, have at least two more relaxing swigs, and go on to putting the wheel back on the bike.

Replacing the repaired wheel is simple if it is a front one. Just make sure the quick-release lever or big axle nuts are loose, then slide the wheel into the forks and tighten (cl) the nuts or push the lever tight (on the left side, of course), checking to see that the rim is centered between the brake shoes as you do the tightening up. If you had to loosen the brakes to get the tire in or out, tighten them up now, and you're set to go.

Replacing a rear wheel is more of a trick. First make sure the axle nuts are loose or the quick-release lever is in its wide open position. On many bikes, it's even necessary to hold the lever with one hand and the cone thingy on the other side of the wheel with the other, so you can loosen (c-cl) the quick-release unit to make room for slipping the wheel back into its place. If the brakes are tight and it was hard to get the wheel out between them, let the air out of the tire now so it won't hang up on them on its way back in.

Now, get in the squat-behind-the-bike position you assumed to pull the wheel out of the frame. Hold the wheel in your left hand, as you did before, and grab the changer with the other. Pull the changer back a bit, so the chain doesn't sag so much (on three-speeds, there's no changer to grab, so you gotta grab the chain itself and pull it back). Now jockey the wheel into place in front of the changer, so the upper span of chain goes over the smallest sprocket. Then move the wheel up and back into its slots in the frame. If it hangs up on its way into the slots, have a friend fuss with the quick-release or the nuts and washers or the brakes or whatever causes the hang-up. Just keep one hand on the changer and the other on the wheel so you can move the wheel into place.

Slide it as far back as it will go, then line up the tire so it is centered between the chainstays, up forward there near the bottom bracket.

Illustration #15 **TIGHTENING REAR WHEEL IN PLACE**

Now you can move your right hand from the changer up to the wheel where it's centered, and keep it exactly there while you use the left hand to tighten the quick-release lever on the other side of the wheel. Tighten (cl) the big nuts thoroughly with your crescent wrench, if you have those instead of a quick-release lever.

Tighten up the brakes, or pump up the tire again if you had to loosen those things to get the tire in there. If you have a three-speed, screw (cl) the indicator back into the hub all the way, then back it off (c-cl) a quarter turn or so and connect the sleeve, turning it clockwise until it tightens against the locknut. Check the gears to make sure you have three. If you don't, see page 108.

When the bike is back together, take a little ride around to make sure the brakes, gears, and newly inflated tire all work. If they do, feel free to whoop with delight, and have a good time on the rest of your ride. Watch out for glass, though . . .

Tire Soft. This may be due to a very slow leak, or to the natural seepage of air out of a tube. If you have any suspicion at all that your tire is soft, pump it up right now. Riding on soft tires wastes huge amounts of your energy, and tires are more liable to puncture when they're soft than when they're hard. This is especially true of the new high-pressure tires. If you go over bumpy roads on soft high-pressure tires, you can get those nasty "snake bite" type holes from the rim cutting into the tube.

So get a pump that fits well on your type of valve (see tools) and keep the tire pumped up to the right pressure at all times. If you're using a frame pump, the kind with the connector right on the end of the pump, you have to make sure you can hold the pump and the bike wheel steady while you pump, so you don't tear the valve off in your frantic efforts to get the last five pounds of pressure in that tire. Lean the bike against a tree, fence post, or telephone pole, and turn the wheel until the valve is at such a height that you can brace the pump against your left knee while you pump with your right hand. Hold your left hand with your thumb cocked against the rim if you have to for extra stability.

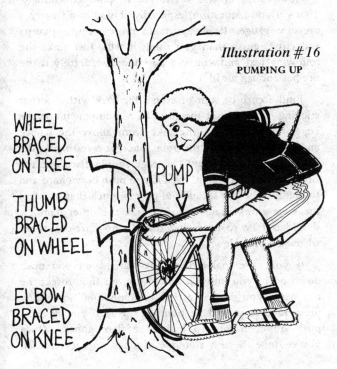

Illustration #16
PUMPING UP

WHEEL
BRACED
ON TREE

PUMP

THUMB
BRACED
ON WHEEL

ELBOW
BRACED
ON KNEE

The point of all this odd posturing and thumb cocking is to keep the pump from jumping and tipping around in relation to the valve. Check to make sure the tire is seated in the rim as you pump it up. The bead should be sunk down into the rim evenly, all the way around. If part of the bead is bulging up and out, STOP pumping, let the air out and work the bead around the rim with your fingers to get it all settled into place. Then you can go back to pumping.

How can you tell when you've pumped enough? That's a good question, especially if you don't carry a pressure gauge. It always takes more pumpa, pumpa and cussa, cussa than you think it will. Just make the following test and you can determine accurately if the tire has enough air in it.

Find a curb or stair or even a big rock with a corner sticking out, and put the tire you're pumping up on the edge. Push down on the bike from above the wheel, and watch the tire at the point where it is resting on the curb edge or whatever. The edge should flare out the tire, but only a tiny bit, even if you push down hard and suddenly. The tire should not give so much that you feel the edge clunk against the rim. On the other hand, it should not be so hard that there is no flare-out at all when you push down.

If your tire makes the little flare when you push down on it, you know it'll hold you up and protect the rim when you go over a rock or something. Some high pressure tires should be pumped up until you have to push quite sharply to make the flare appear. Once you've done the test a couple of times, and gotten used to how hard a push it takes to make your particular tires flare out, you'll be able to tell instantly whether you've got enough pressure in them.

If you don't have a pump, or yours won't get enough pressure in the tire, you can use a gas station air hose, but *be careful!* Many gas stations have compressors that are made to fill truck tires up to 150 pounds per square inch or more. That kind of pressure can blow a bike tire clean away!

Park or lean your bike at the end of the pump island, out of the cars' way, so it is standing up. Spin the tire you need to fill until the valve is down at the bottom of the wheel. That way you can push the "chuck" on the end of the pump hole straight down for a tight, accurate fit. If the chuck is set at an angle, just turn the wheel a bit to get the valve in a convenient place. If you have presta valves, you have to screw the tiny cap up (c-cl), then screw on (cl) an adaptor like the one in illustration 11. Then the end of the hose will fit on your tire.

When everything is set, push the chuck on hard, for just a second. If there is a trigger on the hose, squeeze the trigger as you push the chuck on tight. DON'T let lots of air blast into your tire. Fill the thing a *tiny bit* at a time, letting little squirts of air in, almost like the puffs from a hand pump. Check the tire after every couple of puffs, to make sure it isn't too hard. Watch the bead all around both sides of the rim, too. Don't let it bulge up and away, or it might allow a huge bubble of tube to bloop out and explode in your face. When you think the tire is hard enough, do a careful curb-edge test, as described on the last page, before you ride away.

Hubs

PROBLEMS: *Wheel loose or noisy.* Either your wheel feels loose and unsteady under you, or it rubs constantly against the brakes or frame, or the thing makes cracky-grackly noises. Fix it as much as you can, *now.* You may need more tools to do a good overhaul and adjustment at home, but try to get it halfway functional so you can ride home without destroying the bearings.

If the wheel is noisy, get to a farm or garage, borrow a can of light oil, work some into each side of the hub, and promise yourself to do an overhaul when you get home.

If looseness is the trouble, first see if the wheel is loose in the frame. If you wiggle the wheel with your fingers, does the axle slop around in relation to the drop-out slot in the frame? If so, tighten (cl) your big axle nuts or your quick-release lever.

If you have a quick-release lever and it isn't holding the wheel firmly even when the lever is pushed all the way in, first try swinging the lever around to the other direction to make sure you are pushing it to its tight position and not to the loose extreme.

Loose no matter which way you push it? OK, you have to tighten the unit up. Aim the lever straight out, then grab the little round cone-shaped nut at the other end of the quick-release skewer. It's on the other side of the hub, and if you wiggle the lever end of the skewer, you can see the round nut wiggle over there. Hold the round nut still and turn the lever end clockwise a half turn or so. Then push the lever to its tight position and see if it's holding the wheel firmly. If it's still loose, pull the lever out straight and turn it (cl) again while holding the round nut. It should be pretty hard to lock that lever into its tight position, so the wheel can't jiggle loose.

If your wheel still wiggles when the big axle nuts or quick-release lever are tight, your problem is loose cones. It's hard, and sometimes impossible, to get the cones adjusted right without official Hub Spanners like the one illustrated on page 10. However, if you are stuck on the road and you are afraid your bearings are going to fall out before you get home if you don't do something, you can at least try the procedure below and hope to get things in good enough shape to make it home in one piece. If you have spanners with you, use them, of course, and you can make the adjustment much more accurately and permanently.

Before you try to fiddle around with the bearing unit, first take a close look at it, and at illustration 17, to identify all the parts. You can't see as much of them on your bike as you can in the picture, and at the end of your axle you'll have a big axle nut or quick-

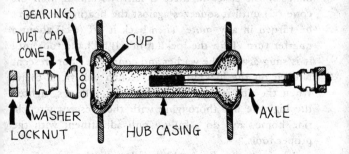

Illustration #17   **HUB, EXPLODED VIEW**

release lever that partially hides the other stuff, but peer behind and around the obstructions and wipe off any grime and grease in there, so you can see the bearing parts, in this order: first a big nut or quick-release lever, then the drop-out of the frame, then a thin locknut, then a washer, and then a cylindrical cone that disappears into the hub and has two slots at its outside edges for a thin spanner. On some three-speed front wheels, there is no thin locknut and washer and all you see is the cone disappearing into the hub.

Know what the parts are on your hub now? Great. The procedure for adjusting the cones will be different, depending on whether you have quick-release levers or not, and depending on whether it's a front or rear wheel you're working on. Find the paragraph below that applies to you and go to it.

If you have a front wheel with big axle nuts, tighten one of them so the wheel will stay in place, and loosen the other. Then reach behind the drop-out with your fingers (you may have to use your baby fingers of both hands if the space in there is narrow) and tighten the cone (cl) until it squeezes against the bearings and can't be turned in any more. Then back it off (c-cl) about a quarter turn. Turn the locknut in (cl) by hand too, until it is snug against the washer and cone. Use your crescent wrench on the locknut if the wrench will fit in there. When the nut is snug against the other things, tighten the big axle nut thoroughly with the crescent wrench, ride home, and do a full-on hub adjustment with the proper tools.

If you have a front wheel with a quick-release lever, pull the lever out and take the wheel off the bike. Then see if either cone-and-locknut set is still tight against itself, so the parts can't be turned around the axle. Get your crescent wrench on the locknut of the tight set, and tighten (cl) the cone on the other side with your fingers. Turn it all the way in (cl) until it squeezes the cone, then back it off (c-cl) about a quarter turn. Now turn the locknut in (cl) until it is snug against the washer and cone. If you have a friend with another wrench, use it to tighten (cl) the locknut, but don't turn it too hard or you might squeeze the whole unit in on the bearings. Put the wheel back in the forks, make sure the quick-release holds the wheel firmly when you push the lever in, and ride home, where you can do a complete hub adjustment with the proper spanners.

If you have a rear wheel with big axle nuts, tighten (cl) the axle nut on the right side of the bike. Next loosen (c-cl) the big axle nut on the left side, where there aren't any sprockets and gear changers in your way. Then use your fingers to tighten (cl) the cone on the left side of the hub in until it is tight against the bearings. You may have to use the baby fingers on both hands to turn the cone in that narrow space in there. On many three-speeds, you won't be able to turn the cone because a square lockwasher holds it still in there; the only thing to do is limp home and do a major adjustment there. But on all other bikes, tighten (cl) the cone all the way in to the bearings, then back it off (c-cl) about a quarter turn. Next turn the locknut in (cl) with your fingers until it is snug against the washer and cone. If you can fit your wrench in there, tighten the locknut with it, but don't do this so much that you tighten the whole unit up on the bearings.

Finally, tighten (cl) the big axle nut with the wrench, then ride home and do a full-on hub adjustment with the proper tools.

If you have a quick-release rear wheel, put the bike in its highest gear, so the chain is on the smallest sprocket, then take the wheel off the bike. See page 45 if you want some hints on how to do this. When you have the wheel off, put your crescent wrench on the locknut that is the only part of the bearing unit showing on the right side of the hub, just visible in the middle of all the sprockets. Then go around to the other side of the hub and tighten (cl) the left cone until it squeezes against the bearings. Back it off (c-cl) a quarter turn or so, then tighten (cl) the locknut with your fingers until it is snug against the washer and cone. If you can get another wrench, use it to tighten the locknut firmly against the washer and cone; just don't turn it in (cl) so hard you tighten up the whole unit. Put the wheel back in the frame, using the hints on page 56 if you need them, then tighten the quick-release lever. Make sure the lever is holding the wheel very firmly in place (it should be pretty hard to push that lever home; if it isn't, see page 62 for the method to tighten up the quick-release mechanism). Ride home and do a complete hub adjustment with the proper spanners before your next ride.

Spokes and Rims

PROBLEMS: *Wheel Bent or Wobbling*. You hit a bad bump, or went into a ditch or something, and one of your wheels is no longer round. The spokes and rims of bicycle wheels are fragile. If some of the spokes are not at the same level of tension as the others, or if some are overstressed by a shock or "side load" of some sort, the wheel will bend. It's no fun to ride on a bent wheel, but if you can get home on it, do so. Truing a wheel properly is a high art. If you want to do it yourself, do it in peaceful, unpressured surroundings, with a good book to help you (see Appendix). Or take the job to a pro.

If, however, you are out on the road and have a wheel that's so bent it won't get you home, here are some things to do in order to get it rolling.

If the wheel is hitting on the brakes, but not the frame, loosen the brakes, with the adjusting barrel or quick-release lever, as shown in illustration 1. This will mean you have to ride home with only one good brake, so be very cautious.

If the rim is bent so badly that the wheel looks like a potato chip, and the tire slams from one side to the other, hitting the brakes and frame stays, you have to resort to drastic methods.

First look at the wheel from above it to get an idea of just how bad the bends are and how many there are. If the whole wheel has been reduced to a cupped-hand shape, so that, for instance, the tire valve and the rim joint opposite the valve may be stuck out to the right side of the bike, while the sections of the rim halfway between those points are both bulging out to the left side, you have a classic sprung wheel. If there is only one section of the wheel bent out to one side from center, with perhaps two small sections on either side bent the other way, you have a rim that's been bent by an impact at one point. Skip the sprung wheel melodrama below, and do the single bend straightening three paragraphs down.

A sprung wheel may well be hopeless. But you can make a last ditch effort if you want. You've got nothing to lose, as long as you don't get so rough you crack the hub.

Let the air out of the tire on the bent wheel, then find a tree or telephone pole that has a root or rock sticking up about a foot out from the base. If you use a rock, pad it with some cloth or a hair net helmet or something, so you don't munch the rim even worse.

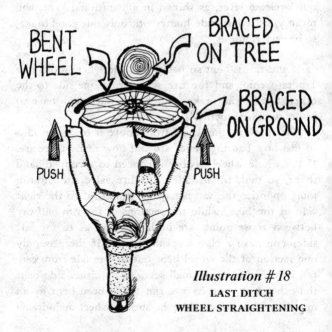

BENT WHEEL

BRACED ON TREE

BRACED ON GROUND

PUSH PUSH

Illustration # 18
LAST DITCH
WHEEL STRAIGHTENING

You can even use a short log braced against the tree if you have to. Just set it up so you have the wheel resting against something solid at the top and the bottom, as shown in illustration 18. Now, the points of the rim that should be braced there are the ones that are bent farthest *away* from you; the points bend toward the tree, in other words. If the top and bottom of the wheel are bent toward you, just turn the bike around so the bends are going the right way. If there are fenders, racks, or other paraphernalia in the way, so you can't set up your wheel like in the illustration, take the wheel off the bike (see page 45 for hints on rear wheel removal), then set it up as shown.

Now put the heels of your hands on the parts of the rim that are bent closest to you and shove, leaning your weight into it. Push gently a couple of times to get the feel of things, then harder once, a sharp shove. This should bend the wheel considerably, and it might even pop it back into a shape that's almost round. If it springs back into its potato chip shape, try again, just a wee bit harder, but not so hard you spring it the other way. Sometimes you can get the thing surprisingly straight. If you do, pump up the tire, wrap any broken spokes around their neighbors to keep them out of trouble, and ride home with a song in your heart. When you get there, you can do a real truing job, or replace the rim, or take the wheel to a pro. If one of the bends comes out of the wheel, but you still have a bend left, or a bend and a couple of secondary bends, fix them according to the method that follows.

If you have a single bend from an impact, or a single big bend with two little ones going the other way on the sides, first see if you can get the wheel somewhere nearer to straight by using a variation on the last ditch effort shown in illustration 18. Turn the wheel so the big bend in it is at the top, and *bent away from you.* If there are mini-bends, they will now be at either side of the big bend, and curving toward you.

Let the air out of the tire and lean the big bend in the wheel against a tree or post. Then just push firmly and sharply with both hands one on either side of the big bend, until you feel the metal give. It may go pretty close to straight the first time you shove, or it may take two or three shoves. Don't push too hard in any case; you don't want to bend the thing the other way, or spring the whole wheel.

When the wheel is a roughly round shape, so it will at least turn around without hitting the frame, you can loosen your brakes and ride it home, then do a good truing job on it, or take it to a pro. Or, if you have a spoke wrench, some time, lots of patience, and a gentle touch with things mechanical, you can try to get it pretty close to round, so you can leave your brakes tight and go on riding. This option will be best for tourists, especially if they have extra spokes along to replace those that break.

Before you start wildly twiddling with the spokes, though, first let out the air in the tire, then spin the wheel and look for "blips" where the wobbles are. A blip is a little outward flare or bump in the rim, caused by hitting a sharp object like the edge of a pothole or a curb. Your brakes will grab on this blip, causing skids and tire wear, so get rid of it if you can. Find a vise-grip tool (don't use any other for this job) at the nearest garage, farm shop, or gas station. The tool is so common you shouldn't have much trouble finding one, unless you're in the middle of the Gobi Desert. I found one in Bogota, Colombia, in about twenty minutes when I was riding through there. Open the jaws of the tool and adjust the knob at the end of one handle so the jaws open wide enough to fit around the width of the rim when the handles of the tool are *clamped shut.* Stick the thing between the spokes of the wheel at the point where you have the blip (see illustration 19). Then center the blip in the jaws of the vise-grip and adjust the jaws so they *just barely* hold onto the blip when the handles of the tool are locked closed.

Now stop. You have, at your fingertips, the potential for the total destruction of the roundness of your rim. Look closely at what you are about to do. Are there blips on both sides of the rim? The vise-grip will squeeze equally from both sides.

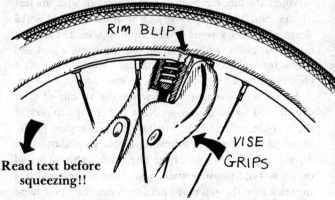

RIM BLIP

Read text before squeezing!!

VISE GRIPS

Illustration #19   **SQUEEZING A BLIP**

If you have a larger blip on one side than the other, squeeze both sides of the rim until the small blip side is flat. Then take a small, thin piece of wood, like a popsicle stick, and put it along the flattened side of the rim. Adjust the jaws of the vise-grip so they accommodate the popsicle stick and the rim when the handles are snapped all the way closed. Then release the little trip lever that's on one of the handles, and, as you keep the jaws barely gripping the rim with one hand, tighten (cl) the adjusting knob of the vise-grip so the jaws move closer to the rim. Turn the knob about one-half of a turn and squeeze the handles together. Watch the rim, looking at it from a tangent. If the blip is still sticking out, tighten the vise-grip adjusting knob again, one-half of a turn or less, and squeeze slowly. Watch out as you squeeze. Stop squeezing if you're going to bend the rim in too far before the vise-grip locks. *Keep in mind that you cannot unsqueeze the rim!*

When the blip has been squeezed in even with the rest of the rim, don't be surprised if there are two small dents on either side of where the blip was. They won't hurt your braking like the blip did. Spin the wheel and check for wobbles. A wobble often comes along with a blip, much as a headache follows a knot on your noggin.

To fix a *minor wobble,* first let the air out of your tire, if you haven't already. Next tighten the brakes, if the wobble isn't already hitting one brake shoe or the other. If you have an adjusting sleeve (see illustration 4), use it. If you don't have one, find a chip of wood or a good old popsicle stick, apply the brakes, and jam the stick into the gap that opens between the brake hand lever and the top of the post (see illustration 3), so the

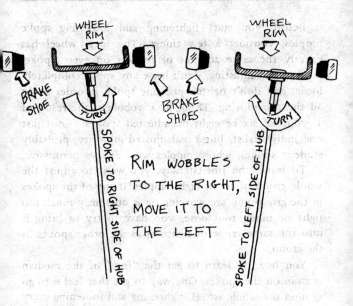

Illustration #20
STRAIGHTENING A MINOR WOBBLE

brake shoes are held in where they'll just touch the rim at the wobble.

Now, to get the wheel closer to straight, you want to move the section of the rim that's hitting the brake shoe away from it. This is done by alternately tightening and loosening a bunch of spokes. For instance, to move the rim to the *left*, *tighten* (cl) the nipples of the spokes that go to the *left* side of the hub, and *loosen* (c-cl) the nipples of the spokes that go to the *right* side of the hub (see illustration 20).

Before you start tightening and loosening spoke nipples, consider a few things. The ideal wheel has exactly the same amount of tension on every spoke. So, in your adjusting, don't leave any spoke completely loose, and don't tighten just one spoke in order to do all the rim moving. Think of a wobble as the result of a group of six or eight maladjusted spokes — not just one individualist, but a maladjusted minority, probably student spokes, whose nipples were always permissive.

To move the rim laterally, you want to adjust the whole group of six or eight nipples. If any of the spokes in the group you are working on is obviously much too tight or much too loose, you have to try to bring it into the same range of tightness as the other spokes in the group.

You have to learn to get the "feel" of the median tension on the spokes. One way to get that feel is to go around the whole wheel, tightening and loosening every spoke about one-tenth of a turn. You might find, right away, that all or most of the nipples are rusty and frozen to the spokes, so they're really hard to turn. If your wheel has frozen nipples (a very uncomfortable condition, I'm sure), use the last ditch straightening method on page 68 and try to get the thing round enough to carry you home, then take it to a pro. If you try to fix it with your spoke wrench out on the road, you'll probably just break a bunch of spokes or strip the flats off the nipple (that sounds uncomfy, too).

Even on a wheel with spoke nipples that turn freely, you will find variations in the tension of the spokes. This is especially true of rear wheels. The rear wheels of most ten-speeds are flattened or "dished" to compensate for the sprockets being on one side. Look down on your rear wheel from above and you'll see how the spokes go out farther on the left than they do on the right. If the wheel is made just right, this won't mean that those right spokes are too tight, but in many cases, I'm sad to say, the right spokes have been cinched in extra tight to dish the wheel.

So when you work on the rear wheel, you'll often find that half the spokes are much tighter than others, and you have to accept their tightness when fixing a wobble. Even on a front wheel you may find some spokes tight, to make up for an imperfection in the rim or something.

The whole point is, don't try to make the wheel perfect. Just work to create a lateral movement of the rim, to make it closer to straight and usable, without putting too much or way too little tension on any one spoke.

Twiddle the spokes at your wobble a bit at a time, loosening the ones to the same side of the hub as the wobble and tightening the spokes to the opposite side of the hub from the wobble, as in illustration 20. Adjust the whole group of six or eight spokes then check to see how much you've improved things. Be careful you don't generate secondary wobbles on the ends of your original wobble. Tighten and loosen more in the middle of the wobble than at the ends. If you get the wobble close enough to straight so the wheel will spin freely between the brake shoes, don't try to take things any further. Ride home and do a finished job, or take it to a pro.

If you begin to have trouble with your one big wobble becoming several bothersome small ones, try again with lots of patience. If your patience is running out, *quit now* and go get a drink of water or a bite to eat or something. If you don't, those spokes can start playing tricks on you. Wobbles appear magically where moments before there was only straightness. One big wobble turns into three little ones. That sort of thing. It can get like the scene in *Fantasia* with Mickey Mouse and the multiplying brooms.

With a great deal of experience, you will learn that elusive "feel" of spoke tension that controls all these secondary wobbles. But if you are new to the game, and stuck out on the road somewhere, just try to get the wheel round enough to carry you home.

Before you pump your tire up on your useably round wheel, check for spoke ends sticking up through the rim. Put a finger under the tire and under the rubber or cloth rim strip that's in there, and run it all the way around the wheel. If there are spoke ends sticking up more than 1/16 of an inch, take the wheel off the bike, take the tire off the wheel, and take care of those sharp spoke ends as explained on page 50.

Broken Spokes. These are most common on tours, when your bike is carrying a heavy load. If you have one on a short ride, and the wheel doesn't have too bad a wobble, or you can get the wobble fairly straight by using the method on page 74, just wrap the broken spoke around one of its neighbors to keep it from snagging in things, and ride home, where you can do a correct replacement, or have it done by a good wheel-builder.

If you are on tour and have a spoke wrench, correct-size spokes, and a freewheel remover (all these things are in the maxi-kit — see page 8) you can replace broken spokes on the road. It's a pain, but you should do it if you can; if you don't, the weakened wheel will probably bend and wobble more and more, breaking spokes and tearing up your brakes as it disintegrates.

First take the wheel off the bike and take the tire off the rim, as on pages 45-46. Take the broken spoke or spokes out of the hub and rim. If you have a ten-speed rear wheel, chances are the broken spokes are on the side of the hub that's blocked by the cluster of sprockets on your freewheel. Some modern freewheel sprockets have matching oval holes in them, so you can neatly slide the spokes out without removing the free-wheel. If you don't have that kind of sprocket, though, and you need to get spokes in and out of the right side of your rear wheel hub, go to page 107 and get the free-wheel off, then come back here for your spoke replacement.

When you have the broken spoke and its nipple re-moved from the rim, take a new spoke in hand and line it up next to one that's already on the wheel to make sure it's the right length. If the head of the spoke is even with the hole in the hub, the other end of it, the one with the threads, should just reach the rim.

Push the new spoke into the hub so it goes through the hole in the same way the old one did. The spokes that go through the hub-holes on either side should be the other way around. For instance, if the head of your spoke winds up on the outside of the hub flange, the two adjacent spokes should have their heads on the inside of the flange. Draw the new spoke through the maze of others, and get it so it's pointing straight out at the rim, without touching any of those other spokes. You may have to curve the spoke a little to get it woven through there, but that's OK. It'll straighten out when it's tightened as long as you don't put a sharp bend in it.

When you have drawn the spoke all the way through, so its head is seated against the hub flange, it will not be pointing at the hole for it. To get it aimed at its hole, first look at the two spokes whose heads are on either side of yours in the hub flange. These spokes will both run out to the rim in the same direction, either forward or back. The spokes must alternate, so if the two spokes on the sides of yours go forward, make yours go back, or vice versa. Move your spoke end through its brothers, like a dancer weaving through a Virginia Reel, until it points at the hole in the rim. It should be able to barely stick into that hole, or at least come quite close to sticking into it.

Now check to see if the other spokes on the wheel are "laced." On almost all bikes, the spokes cross each other several times on the way out to the rim. On laced wheels (which most good bikes have), the spokes touch at the point where they cross nearest to the rim. This makes the wheel more stable in the horizontal plane, and also means that when a road shock comes up a spoke, it travels through the cross into a second spoke, so it is absorbed twice as well. If your wheel is laced, make sure you weave the new spoke through the old ones to match the lacing of the other spokes around the wheel.

Insert the nipple through the hole for your new, correctly laced spoke. Spin the nipple onto the spoke and tighten it with your fingers. Turn to page 54 so you can get your tire back on the rim and your wheel back in the bike. Then true the wheel, as explained on page 74, making sure the new spoke gets into the same range of tightness as the ones around it. That way the wheel won't be overstressed any more, and if you ride carefully, you probably won't break any more spokes on your trip.

Do a first rate truing job when you get to a stopover, or have a pro do it, so the spokes' tension will be at optimum balance for wheel strength.

7
Seat or Saddle

PROBLEMS: *Seat Loose.* If it *tilts forward and back* on the end of the seat post, get your crescent wrench set so it will fit the nuts on the tightening bolt EXACTLY, then tighten them up (cl). Tighten them evenly, doing a few turns on one, then a few on the other. As you tighten, shift the seat slightly every once in a while to make sure it is settling into the right grooves in the mounting bracket to hold the position that's most comfortable for you. It should be very close to level at any rate. When the nuts get hard to tighten, make double sure the wrench is adjusted to fit tight each time you put leverage on it. Don't tighten so much the bolt shears off, but get each nut so tight that you can feel it straining hard on its threads. That way the nut will stay tight, and hopefully, the seat won't slip up and down. If it does in spite of your best efforts, you have to ride all the way home trying to stay gingerly balanced on the thing, then replace the bracket with a new one that doesn't have all the little bumps worn off. I recommend the micro-adjustable post-bracket units, like the SR Laprade. They never lose their grip on the seat if you tighten them up properly.

If your *seat swivels from side to side,* or the whole post slides down into the frame tube so the seat is too low, first loosen (c-cl) the binderbolt or binderbolt nut with your crescent wrench, or allen wrench if needed. Then set the post so the seat is at the right height for you. I'm not going to tell you what your right height is. Generally, though, people like the seat set at such a

level that when they sit on it, they can put the pedal
at the bottom of its stroke, stretch their leg out straight,
and rest their heel flat on the pedal. Measure pedal
length with *your* seater centered on the bike seat so
that as you pedal down the road *your* seater doesn't
have to rock from side to side on the bike seat, thus
creating that distressing friction. When you get the seat
where you want it, tighten (cl) the binderbolt or binderbolt nut with your crescent wrench, making sure it fits
precisely so you don't round off the nut. If you have
the kind of binderbolt that needs an allen wrench to be
tightened, use your allen wrench and don't be afraid to
turn hard on the little thing, sticking the short end of
the "L" shape into the little hex-hole and pushing hard
on the long end of the tool.

You have to really tighten that binderbolt well in
order to keep the seat in place. So be firm, but careful.
If you can get to a farm shop or garage that has oil,

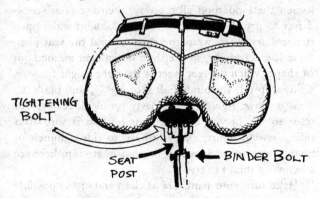

TIGHTENING
BOLT

SEAT
POST

BINDER BOLT

Illustration #21   **THE SEAT**

it's best to put a drop on the threads of the binderbolt before you tighten it up (cl).

If no amount of patient tightening on the binderbolt will tighten up the frame tube enough to hold the seat post still, you must have a post that's too small for your frame tube. Not to worry, there's still something you can do, even if you're out on the road. Find an aluminum beer or soda pop can (they're all too easy to find along the roads around here) and cut out a rectangular piece of it that's about 1 inch by 2½ inches. Cut the edges as clean as you can, and smooth off any burrs or bumps at the edges by wrapping the piece of aluminum around your seat post, rubbing the edges flat with the edge of the handle of your crescent wrench or something, then using the little piece of sandpaper in your tire patch kit to get the edges nice and smooth.

This curved, smooth-edged piece of aluminum can be used as a "shim" to make your seat post wider. Just loosen the binderbolt all the way, then use your screwdriver to pry the top of the frame tube a bit wider open if necessary, then wrap the shim around the seat post. Slide it in carefully, so the shim doesn't get mashed out of shape. When the seat is set at the right height for you, tighten up (cl) the binderbolt thoroughly, and that's it.

Seat hurts. Agh. This is a nasty problem. It does not refer to the bicycle seat. If your bottom is sore after riding several hours, and you have to ride a bunch of hours more to get home or to your next stop, here are a bunch of things to try.

Make sure your pants are as clean and dry as possible where you sit, and that they don't get bunched up under there. Tight cycling shorts with a clean chamois in the crotch are best. You can clean the chamois off at night with alcohol, and it'll be ready to use the next morning. Clean tight corduroy shorts and thin cotton underpants are OK, too, but they have to be changed often.

Adjust the bike seat so it's close to level and neither too high nor too low, then change your hand position on the handlebars often, so you can sit in different places, forward and back, resting your weight on different parts of that tender region of your anatomy.

If the seat is a leather one and it has gotten all hard and dried out by the weather, get some kind of softening stuff, like saddle soap or mink oil or even neat's foot oil. Either of the former two can be used on the top of the saddle, but they should be used sparingly. Neat's foot oil must be used on the underside of the seat, or it will soak into your shorts and stain them, and eventually get to your skin and start having weird and uncomfortable effects on it, akin to the effects it has on the tanned skin of the cow.

If the seat is a plastic one there is very little you can do to make it more comfortable. Plastic seats either fit you or they don't. If you are on a long tour and your plastic seat hurts, the best thing you can do is head for a good bike shop and see if they have a seat with a strong nylon "shell" and anatomic padding bulges where your two pelvic bones rest. The seat should be thin and unpadded toward the front, though, so you don't chafe your thighs there. If you can get one of these anatomically padded seats that fits you OK, you'll be much better off for the rest of your tour than if you kept going on the seat that hurt, or bought a fancy leather one and had to break it in as you rode.

8
Power Chain

DIAGNOSIS: The power train is what should deliver your pedal power to the rear wheel. The front half of the system consists of the pedals, the cranks, the bottom bracket set, the front chainwheels (sprockets), and on a ten-speed, a front changer (derailleur). Between the front and back halves of the power train runs a messy, oily chain. The back half of the system consists of the rear sprockets (on a freewheel) and either a three-speed hub or a rear changer (derailleur). When you have any problem with the whole system, first find out which half of the power train is acting up, then zero in on the individual part that's ailing and fix the thing. Don't just fiddle with any part that comes to mind; you may spend hours before you start solving your actual problem.

If at any time you have a power train problem you can't solve out on the road, there is a way to get home on your crippled bike, as long as you have a cycling friend and a spare tire or tube along. Simply loop your spare over your friend's seat post, and hold onto it so he or she can tow you. If the two of you are about the same size, you should offer to do the towing end of the deal for at least half the distance. I've come many miles out of the deep woods sharing the tow-tube with Bryan, my main cycling companion.

If there are nasty *grinding, rubbing, squeaking, ker-chunking, clinking,* or *clunking noises* when you pedal, make this easy test to find out if you have a power train problem. Get going at a good clip on a quiet, level place or a slight downhill grade, then coast and listen. If the nasty noises do not stop when you stop pedaling, your problem is in a wheel, not the power train. See Hub PROBLEMS and check for brake *stickies* (page 13) too.

If a nasty noise appears only when you pedal, see if it repeats itself, and how often. If it repeats once each time your pedal makes a revolution, then it's probably a Front Half problem. If it repeats itself approximately once for every two revolutions of your pedal, then you have a chain problem; go directly to Chain PROBLEMS (page 103). If the noise repeats two to three times for every revolution of the pedal, you probably have a

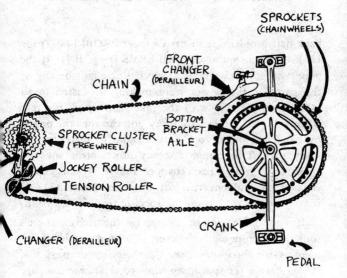

SPROCKETS
(CHAINWHEELS)

FRONT
CHANGER
(DERAILLEUR)

CHAIN

BOTTOM
BRACKET
AXLE

SPROCKET CLUSTER
(FREEWHEEL)

JOCKEY ROLLER

TENSION ROLLER

CRANK

CHANGER (DERAILLEUR)

PEDAL

Illustration #22   **TEN-SPEED POWER TRAIN**

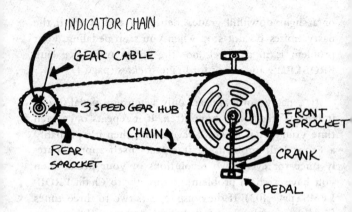

Illustration #23   **THREE-SPEED POWER TRAIN**

back half problem; see Rear Changer PROBLEMS (page 126) and Rear Sprocket PROBLEMS (page 107). If the noise you get is constant, unvarying, it might be any of the parts of the power train making it. Listen to all of them, preferably with the bike held up so the rear wheel's off the ground; that way you can turn the pedals by hand and move your head around to listen for the noisy part. Two common steady noises are a squeaky chain and grindy rear changer rollers. When you've isolated the problem area, turn to the section that covers it so you can zero in on the specific trouble and fix it.

If your *gears slip* or change by themselves, there's something wrong with the control lever or cable adjustment. On a three-speed, see *Gear slippage* on page 108. If you have a ten-speed, see *slippage or stickies* on page 112.

If you have a ten-speed and the chain keeps coming off the front sprockets, or makes noise against the front changer, or if you can't get the chain onto one of the front sprockets, see Front Changer PROBLEMS on page 115. If the chain comes off the rear sprockets, see the Rear Changer PROBLEMS on page 119.

If you hear a plunk-plunking noise when you're in low gear and the chain is on the largest of the rear sprockets, STOP RIDING!!! That innocuous little sound is a warning that the rear changer (derailleur) is out of adjustment, and about to self-destruct in the rear wheel spokes. See Rear Changer *adjustment* on page 121 to save the thing from certain death.

Front Half of Power Train

DIAGNOSIS: If you have a problem with the front half of your power system, you have to find out where it is, then go to the section on that unit. If your chain is throwing, or the front gears slip, or your front changer rubs on the chain all the time, see Front Changer PROBLEMS, on page 115 with the rest of the stuff on changers.

If your chain goes *kerchunk* and jumps up each time it hits a certain point of the front sprocket, see Front Sprocket PROBLEMS. If you hear nasty noises, like clicks, clunks, or harsh squeaks at each revolution of the pedal, first check the pedal itself. Is it hard to revolve on its spindle by hand? Is it loose on the spindle? Is it obviously bent or bashed? When you spin it by hand, does it catch and stick? Has the dust cap come off so dirt can get into the bearings (see illustration 24)? For any of these symptoms, see Pedal PROBLEMS.

If you hear a clunk or sharp squeak each time you push down on one pedal or the other, or if you sometimes feel a slight slippage of a pedal as you push hard on it, or if one of the cranks is knocking on the frame or the kickstand each time it passes, see Cranks.

If you hear grinding noises that you can't pin down on the pedals, or if your whole front half can slip back and forth and wiggle in the frame, or if the whole front half is hard to turn, then see Bottom Bracket.

PEDALS

PROBLEMS: *Pedals loose or tight and noisy.* First make sure the spindle is screwed tightly into the crank. If it's loose, you need to get a wrench that'll fit tight on those two flats that are on the spindle right next to where it screws into the crank. Your crescent may fit in there, or the space may be too small. If it is, you can use a strong cone wrench (take it easy so you don't bend the thing) if you've got one with you. Or you can find a shop that has a flat, open end, 15 mm or 9/16 inch pedal

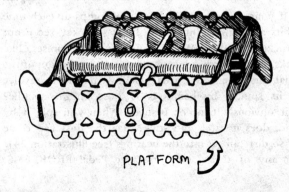

PLATFORM ↖

spanner. If you can't find any of those things, use some narrow-jawed or needlenose pliers to get the spindle a little bit tighter than it was, then keep an eye on the pedal as you limp to the nearest good bike shop for a pedal spanner.

If you've got a good wrench for your pedal, tighten it thoroughly. Remember that the left pedal tightens *counter-clockwise,* or backwards. The right pedal tightens clockwise, like most other threaded parts on your bike.

If the pedal has a dust cap over the outer end of the spindle, see if it is loose enough to take off with your hands or a pair of wide pliers or something. Look inside. If you can wiggle the pedal back and forth on the spindle, back off (c-cl) the locknut on the end of the spindle by sticking your crescent wrench jaws in there end-wise. Then tighten (cl) the cone by sticking the screwdriver in and pushing it around until it catches on the little flats of the cones. Twist the cone (cl) until it is tight on the bearings, then back it off (c-cl) a half turn. Then tighten (cl) the locknut. Put a drop of oil

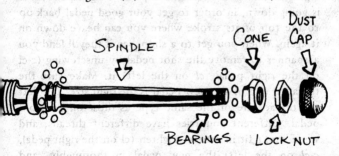

Illustration #24   **PEDAL, EXPLODED VIEW**

in there and try to get a drop into the bearings at the other end of the pedal too. If the pedal is tight (hard to turn), adjust the cone to make it a little looser (c-cl). As with all bearings, these should be set so there is very little "play" or wiggle-room; just enough to let the little balls roll around freely.

If you don't have a locknut and cone unit under the dust cap, your pedal doesn't have ball bearings, and you can't adjust it. You have to limp home or to the nearest bike shop and replace the whole pedal with one that's got good bearings. Shops will often lend you their pedal spanner to put the new one on, or put it on for you. Just make sure the spindle of your new pedal has the same size and type threads as your old one, and remember that the left pedal tightens *counterclockwise* instead of clockwise like the right one.

Pedal bent, bashed, or broken. You have to limp home or to a bike shop as well as you can. In many cases you can use the other foot to do the work of pedaling, and just give the mashed pedal a light push as it is going down, in order to get your good pedal back up to the top of its stroke where you can heave down on it again. When you get to a shop, see if they'll lend you a spanner to remove the shot pedal by unscrewing (c-cl on the right pedal, *cl* on the left) it. Make sure the threaded end of the new pedal is the right size, and that the threads are of the same type as those on your old pedal. Different countries have different threads, and some won't fit in others. Tighten (cl on the right pedal, c-cl on the left) the new pedal in thoroughly, and you're on your way.

CRANKS

PROBLEMS: *Clunk or sharp squeak* heard at each revolution of the pedal. You may not hear anything, and still feel slight slippage each time you push down on one of the pedals. Your *crank is loose* where it attaches to the thick axle that goes through the bottom bracket in the frame. Don't ride the bike with a loose crank! Especially you cotterless crank people. You may have to hobble to a farm shop, garage, or bike shop, using only the tight crank to pedal, but don't use the loose one or you'll mess it up so much you'll have to buy a new crank.

To check to make sure a loose crank is your problem, and to find out which one is loose, get off the bike and lean it against a wall, then put the pedals so they are one forward, one back, with the cranks horizontal. Get the weight of your body suspended over the pedals and put your hands down on them, one on each. This may require sticking your shoulder through the diamond of the frame. When you're all set, push down sharply on both pedals at the same time with your hands, putting all your weight behind the push. Feel anything give? Rotate the cranks 180 degrees and give the pedals another sharp push with your hands. Something give? Watch the joint of each crank and the bottom bracket axle as you push down in order to determine which crank is loose. To tighten up a loose crank, the procedure is different, depending on whether it is cottered or cotterless. If it's the heavy ashtabula type, it can't be loose; both cranks and the bottom bracket axle are one piece.

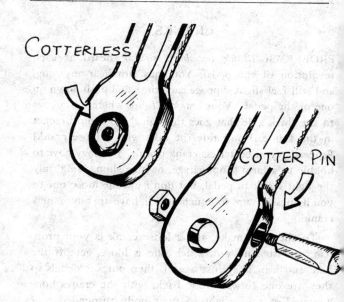

Illustration #25
CRANKS

To *tighten a cotterless crank* you need a special socket-type tool that fits into the shallow hole in the crank and tightens (cl) the bolt or nut in there. This squeezes the crank onto the square end of the bottom bracket axle. If you don't have a special tool along with you, find somebody with a fine-quality metric socket set. This may seem like an invitation to a wild goose chase, but in many cases you can find a foreign car mechanic, or a foreign tractor mechanic, who has a socket that'll fit your crank bolt or nut. In some cases you have to find a thin-walled socket, because the shallow hole around the crank bolt is so small a heavy-walled socket won't fit in there. But even out in the boonies, there are now lots of things like efficient little Kubota tractors (the farm version of the Datsun gas-saver) and mechanics with tools to fix them.

When you've found a socket that fits your crank bolt or nut, tighten (cl) the thing thoroughly, making the wrench handle and the crank into a "closing V" shape so you can hold the crank still and lever the wrench handle toward it with the same hand. You can get the bolt or nut very tight by this method. Just make sure you don't do it so hard you strip the threads.

If your *cottered crank is loose,* you have to do a litle Rube Goldberg tool-making to get the thing tight. First try to find something that you can use to hold the back of the bike up off the ground by balancing the whole thing on the loose crank. An 11- or 12-inch high curb (the type that abound in old Western cow towns) is perfect. A big square block of stone or wood that's about a foot high will do too. Next you need a great big nut, or a little (½ inch deep) crack or hole in your bike holder-upper. Then you set the bike up as shown in illustration 26, with the crank resting on the holder-upper or big nut, and the little nut on the end of the cotter pin sticking down inside the half-inch deep crack or inside the big nut, where it won't get bashed around. Then use a hammer or a hard, smooth stone to tap on the rounded end of the cotter pin and drive it in tight. If you can't get a big nut or small hole so you can set things up as in illustration 26, you can rotate the crank forward about 45 degrees, so the little bolt isn't under it any more, then rest the crank on the holder-upper without using a big nut or small crack, and tap on the round end of the cotter at an angle to get it tight. If worse comes to worst, you can tap on the

Illustration #26
TIGHTENING COTTERED CRANK

thing without any holder-upper, but this is risky. You can easily drive the bottom bracket bearings into their races, making a bumpy road for them to run along in, thus ruining the whole bottom bracket set. So use a holder-upper if at all possible.

When the cotter pin has been knocked in tight, take the bike off the holder-upper and tighten (cl) the little nut with your crescent wrench. Don't tighten it hard; it isn't meant to hold the crank on, and the threads strip very easily.

Crank knocking frame of bike. If you've had a wreck and banged one pedal so hard the crank is bent and hits against the chain stay or the kickstand, there isn't too much you can do with your road tools. If the crank just taps the kickstand, see if you can loosen (c-cl) the nut that holds the stand and turn it in farther so the pedal misses. Or take the kickstand off altogether.

If the crank is really whacking the chain stay of the frame, there is a last-ditch method you can try for a temporary fix to get you home. Limp or coast or get a tow (see page 84) so a good farm shop or a garage that has a huge (18 inches or 20 inches) crescent wrench. Then take the pedal off the bent crank (see page 90) and wrap some heavy cloth or burlap around the end of the crank. Then turn the crank so it is pointing straight up, and lay the bike down gently on the other side from the one with the bent crank.

Put the big wrench on the end of the crank, making sure the jaws are lined up so they won't dig into the threaded hole for the pedal spindle. Hold the top tube of the bike down with one hand, and use the other hand to lever the big wrench up, slowly and steadily straightening the crank. If it is a strong crank, it'll take a lot of spaghetti power on that wrench. You may even have to ask a friend to help hold the bike still while you do the bending. But do it slowly, so you don't snap the crank off or bend it too far.

When the crank is fairly close to straight, put the pedal back on, then make a mental note to take the bike to a good shop for professional straightening, or replace the crank when you get home. A bent and rebent crank is much weaker than a new one.

BOTTOM BRACKET

PROBLEMS: *Bottom Bracket Loose or tight.* Either your whole bottom bracket axle is loose so it jiggles from side to side when you pedal, or it is hard to turn the cranks at all. You have to adjust the adjustable bearing race on the left side of the bottom bracket. First take your screwdriver and set the end in one of the notches in the lockring. Tap the screwdriver, aiming it counterclockwise to loosen the ring. When the ring is loose, take the small screwdriver and set one corner of the blade in one of the small holes that are set into the end of the adjustable bearing cup, and turn the thing the way you need to to tighten (cl) or loosen (c-cl) it. The best way is to tighten (cl) it all the way in until it's hard to turn the cranks, then back off (c-cl) the adjustable cup about an eighth of a turn.

If the crank still gets jiggly after a while, your fixed cup is loose. All you can do with it is turn it in with your fingers or a borrowed channel-lock pliers if pos-

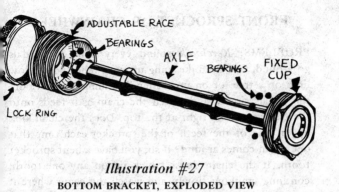

ADJUSTABLE RACE
BEARINGS
AXLE
BEARINGS
FIXED CUP
LOCK RING

Illustration #27
BOTTOM BRACKET, EXPLODED VIEW

sible. The fixed cup tightens clockwise on some bikes, counterclockwise on others, so you have to figure out which works on yours and get it as tight as you can manage, then ride home, keeping an eye on it. Then tighten it up with a tool that fits in there, or take it to a shop that will have the thin, correct-sized spanner to tighten the fixed cup.

Bottom Bracket Noisy: If you have grindy, crackly noises coming from the front half of your power train, and you can't trace them to the pedals or cranks, chances are they are being made by grit or worn parts inside the bottom bracket. See if you can find some fine oil (10-20 weight motor oil or automatic transmission oil) and work a couple of drops into each side of the bottom bracket around the axle. Then ride home and do a complete bottom bracket overhaul, as described in a good fix-it book. Consider buying a sealed-bearing bottom bracket like the Phil Wood one, if you live in a wet, dusty, or sandy area.

FRONT SPROCKET OR CHAINWHEEL

PROBLEMS: *Kerchunk* sound every time the pedals go around. Get the bike hung up on a fence post, a low limb on a tree, or on your friend's willing hands. Crank the pedals slowly and watch the chain as it feeds onto the front sprocket right at the top. Does the chain kick up on one of the teeth of the sprocket each time that one tooth comes around? If so, you have a bent sprocket tooth. If the chain doesn't kick up on any one tooth, continue cranking slowly and watch the chain where it goes through the rollers on the gear changer. Does the chain kick up or jump a little back there every once in a while? Look closely at the chain where it jumps. Is a link of the chain stuck so it doesn't bend and then straighten out? See *Chain Problems* to fix that link. Is the chain kicking up on one tooth of a rear sprocket? See *Rear Sprocket Problems*.

If you have a *bent tooth* on your front chainwheel, you have to play dentist. Mark the tooth that the chain kicks up on. You can just make a fingernail mark in the grease if you don't have a flow-pen.

Take the chain off the chainwheel. On a one- or three-speed bike, you have to loosen (c-cl) the rear wheel axle nuts and slip the wheel forward to get the chain loose enough to slip off the sprocket.

With the chain off, spin the cranks slowly and look down from directly above the front chainwheel. Watch that you don't bonk your chin with a pedal, but also watch closely for the marked tooth as it comes over the top of the chainwheel. Can you see which way it's bent compared to the ones on either side? If you can't see

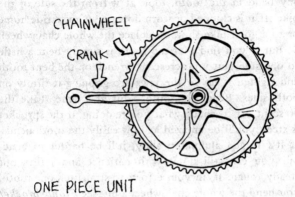

CHAINWHEEL

CRANK

ONE PIECE UNIT

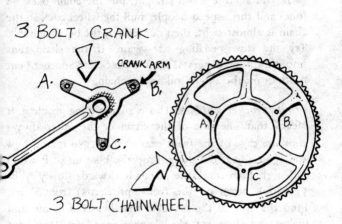

3 BOLT CRANK

A.

CRANK ARM

B.

C.

3 BOLT CHAINWHEEL

A.

B.

C.

Illustration #28

TWO DIFFERENT CHAINWHEELS

any bend in the tooth, look at it from the side of the bike. If it is chipped or worn down, you gotta ride home or to a good bike shop to replace the whole chainwheel.

But if you find that the tooth is simply bent a little to one side, put your crescent wrench on the bent tooth and tighten it up so the jaws are gripping it firmly on both sides. Bend the tooth a bit at a time. Take the crescent off to check what you're doing. If the sprocket is steel, you'll be amazed at how easily the tooth bends. If it's forged aluminum alloy, it'll be harder to bend, but you can still do it with patience and a firm but steady touch. If, in your efforts to straighten one tooth, you bend the whole chainwheel a bit, see *Front sprocket wobbles,* below.

If you get the tooth straight, put the chain back on (one- and three-speed people, pull the wheel back so the chain is almost tight, then tighten (cl) the big axle nuts). Try the slow pedaling test again. If the chain runs smoothly now, congrats! If not, check for another bent tooth or maybe a tight link in the chain.

Front sprocket wobbles. This is an annoying problem. It means that one side of the chain or the other always rubs the cage of the front gear changer. No matter how well you adjust the thing. Prop the bike up so it won't fall over, then crank the pedals backwards slowly while you look down on the front sprocket(s) from above. Find the area of the sprocket that bends in or out and makes the chain rub the changer cage. Mark the bent area of the sprocket, with some grease from the chain if you don't have anything better to do it with. Sometimes it's hard to tell whether the sprocket is bent in on one

de or out on the other. Try to decide where the major-
y of the sprocket is, and call the rest bent. Does the
ent area you marked fall near one of the crank arms
hat hold the chainwheel to the crank? Usually a bent
procket has been caused by a bent crank arm or a bad
onnection between the arm and the sprocket (see illus-
ration 28).

Make sure all the bolts that hold the sprocket to the
rank arms are tight. They're all tight and you still have
wobble? OK. The only way you can get the thing
traight is to whack it with something. Get a hammer
nd a block of hardwood that's about 2 by 4 by 6 inches
f you can. Or get a smooth round rock and any piece
f wood that'll butt up against the side of the crank
rm where your bend is. Put the block on the side of the
procket you want to bend back, then give the block a
olid slug with your rock or hammer. You may have to
ay the bike down gently on one side to get a good
lug. Check to see if you've straightened the chainwheel
fter your first slug. Rotate the chainwheel if you have
o take a second slug, so you don't wreck the bottom
racket bearings. If you don't get the chainwheel per-
ectly straight, don't worry about it; if it's good enough
o it doesn't make the chain rub on the gear changer
very time it goes around, you've done a good job.
Ride on in peace.

Chain

PROBLEMS: *Chain thrown*. That means your chain has
come off one or both of the sprockets. If you have a ten-
speed, you probably need to adjust your gear changers.

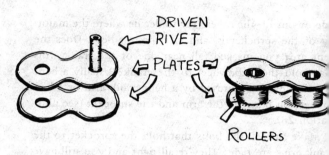

Illustration #29
TWO DIFFERENT CHAIN LINKS

But use this section to get your chain back on and to check the chain for looseness and lack of oil too.

If the chain is jammed on either side of the free-wheel sprockets, you have to grab (yuch!) the upper section of chain, just forward from those rear sprockets, then yank up as you slowly rotate the rear wheel forward. If the chain threw off the highest (smallest) gear, you may have to loosen the rear wheel axle nuts or quick-release to free the jammed chain.

To get your chain back on the bike, put it on the rear sprocket first. Ten-speed people, put the rear changer in its high gear position (all the way forward), then see that the chain goes through both of the small rollers, making a backwards "S" shape. Get it to run from the top roller onto the smallest sprocket, and all the way around that sprocket so it goes straight forward from the top.

When the chain is set on the rear sprocket, pull the length of chain that comes off the top of the rear sprocket tight, and press a couple of links down over the teeth at the top of the front sprocket. Crank the pedals forward while holding those links on the sprocket teeth (you have to walk along next to the bike as it rolls forward) and the rest of the chain will pop onto the sprocket.

Read the rest of the PROBLEMS in this Chain section and find out what made the chain jump off. If the chain is AOK, check your gear changer adjustment, and front and rear sprockets, for wobbles or kerchunking teeth.

Squeaky or gunky chain. You haven't oiled or cleaned it in a while. It's easy to forget. But you pay heavily for that negligence on a long ride; a dry or dirty chain uses up a lot of your energy.

Before oiling the chain, see how dirty it is. You might want to get some solvent from a garage or farm shop, put it on a rag, and run the pedals backwards with the chain sliding through the cleaning rag. This'll take enough of the gunk off to make the chain useable.

To oil the chain, get a can of light (10 to 20 weight oil with a thin spout — gas stations and home shops usually have an oil can around someplace) and hold it over the front of the front sprocket, so the oil will drip down onto the chain at its frontmost point. Crank the pedals backwards slowly and dribble the oil from roller to roller as they come up at you. Go easy on the oil; it only takes one drop on each roller.

When you have oil on every single roller, take a rag, squirt a little on it, and spread it around, into a big blotch. Then hold the rag wrapped around the lower section of chain, the part that's stretched between the bottom of the front and rear sprockets. Rotate the cranks to spread an even, thin film of oil all over the chain. Don't leave lots of extra oil on there; it attracts grit, which can raise the coefficient of friction higher than the oil lowers it. Especially if you ride near the beach where that oil picks up sand.

When you get back on the bike you'll notice an incredible improvement in the ease of pedaling, especially on level terrain. Remember that. Keep the chain covered with its nice, thin coat of oil at all times. Check it often during wet weather to make sure the coat doesn't get washed off.

Loose chain. Your chain sags down between the front and rear sprockets, and tends to fall off them.

On a three-speed, you have to move the rear wheel back to tighten the chain. Loosen (c-cl) the big axle nuts that hold the rear wheel to the bike frame. Pull the rear wheel back until the chain is tight, then ease it forward just a hair. The chain should be tight enough so that if you grab a link of it that's halfway between the front and rear sprockets, you can move it up and down only about a half inch. It should *not* be as tight as a G string on a banjo; if it is, it may ruin the rear hub bearings. When the chain is set at the right tension, align the wheel so the tire is centered between the chainstays of the frame, then tighten (cl) the big axle nuts.

If a *ten-speed chain is loose*, it will sag down between the front and rear sprockets when the changers are set so the chain is in the small (low gear) front sprocket, and the smaller (high gear) rear sprockets. The problem is that the rear changer can't take up all the slack chain. See how tight the chain is when you shift both changers to the large sprocket positions. If that doesn't make the chain so tight that it yanks the rear changer forward to a horizontal position, you can take a link out of the chain if you have a chain tool. I don't recommend doing this on the road, though. You might wreck the chain. Then you're *really* stuck. Better to ride home or to a shop with your saggy chain, then take your time and do the link removal with a good tool.

Tight link. When one part of your chain goes over a roller or a sprocket, particularly a small rear sprocket, the chain kinks. When the same part of the chain comes off the sprocket, it doesn't come unkinked. If you suspect that you have a tight link, get the bike up on a rack and crank the pedals slowly. Watch the chain as it goes over the rear sprocket, or in the case of a ten-speed, through the rollers on the rear changer (see illustration 22). Does the chain jump a little each time one link comes around? That's your tight link. You can find the one for sure by flexing the jumpy area of the chain with your fingers until you find the one that doesn't want to flex. When you have found the tight link, mark it with a little scratch on the side plate so you don't lose it among its brothers.

Try to loosen the tight link up with a little oil first. Work the oil in by flexing the link with your fingers, not only up and down, but from side to side, so you can loosen up the joints between the rivets and the rollers.

Look closely at the tight link and the ones around it. Is there a twist in the chain at your tight link? If so, get two crescent wrenches (you *are* riding with a friend who's got one, I hope) and adjust the wrenches carefully so they are squeezing the side plates of the links to either side of the twisted one. Then twist the wrenches gently, against the bend, to straighten it out. It's amazing how often you can get the thing pretty close to straight, or at least straight enough to loosen the link and get home without throwing your chain a thousand times.

If you have a chain tool and you can't get your tight link loose by any of the above methods, set the rivet of the tight link in the slot on the chain tool that's for spreading links (this slot will be closest to the twisting handle) and CAREFULLY push the rivet in with the point of the tool. Make sure the point is centered on the rivet end when it pushes, and make sure you spread the link plates only a hair or two. That'll be enough to loosen them from the roller, but not enough to pop the plates off the rivet.

When you've fixed your tight link, oil the rest of the links (see *Squeaky chain*) so no others tighten up on you.

Chain worn, or lots of kerchunking. Your chain has seen a lot of hard service, and maybe you replaced the rear sprockets but not the chain. The chain is probably so worn and stretched that it won't fit onto the sprocket teeth properly, so it jumps and kerchunks every time you pedal hard. To make sure it is a worn chain causing the trouble, just pull on one of the links that are wrapped around the front of the front sprocket. If the chain pulls away from the sprocket until you can see the end of a tooth under it, your chain is worn out and must be replaced. Oil it if it's dry, and ride home or to a bike shop, using your large front sprocket and large to middle rear sprockets, to avoid kerchunking and throwing the chain as much as possible.

Back Half of Power Train

REAR SPROCKETS

PROBLEMS: *Kerchunk*. Your chain kicks up about twice to every revolution of the pedals. It makes a most annoying jerk if you're pedaling hard. Check first to make sure the kerchunk isn't due to a faulty chain or front sprocket. If it's the freewheel that's worn, the best thing to do is ride home without pushing too hard, then take your time to remove the freewheel there, and get a replacement, and a new chain at the same time, so your whole power train will be a matched unit. If you're on a long tour and have a freewheel remover tool (see page 11) that fits the slots or notches in your freewheel, ride to a shop. If they won't do the removal and replacement on the spot, you can do it yourself.

First remove the rear wheel (see page 45 for hints), then take the big axle nut off the freewheel side of the wheel, or unscrew (c-cl) the quick-release skewer (hold the lever in one hand, and the cone-shaped nut at the other end with the other hand) Put the remover tool in place, making sure it fits all the way down into the notches or slots. You may have to take off the locknut of the bearing set (see illustration 17) to get your remover tool all the way into place. Put the big axle nut or the quick-release skewer (without its little springs) back on the wheel and tighten (cl) it down on the remover, then back it off (c-cl) just a bit. Get a big

wrench on the remover tool, or put the thing in a vise
with the wheel resting on top of it, then undo the freewheel. It may take some real grunting. Just make sure
you don't tear the slots out of the freewheel or bend
the wheel in your excitement.

Put the new freewheel on VERY carefully, after
dabbing a little grease on the aluminum threads of the
hub. Those threads are extremely delicate. Start turning
the freewheel on by hand, and if it gets hard to turn
at all, take it off and start over, being super careful
not to strip the threads. When you have the freewheel
on, replace the big axle nut or quick-release skewer
and springs (the small ends of the springs should point
toward the center of the hub) and put the wheel back in
the bike. If you replace the chain at the same time you
put on your new freewheel, you won't have any kerchunking for a long time.

GEAR CHANGERS

DIAGNOSIS: As with brakes, gear changer systems
are made up of three units: the lever, the cable, and the
changer or derailleur mechanism itself. Different problems are liable to be caused by each of the different
units.

Hub Changer

PROBLEMS: *Gear Slippage or loss.* Your middle gear,
the one you ride in most of the time, suddenly loses
grip. Your feet fall off the pedals, and you make a painful landing on the top tube of the bike. Agh. You may
discover your loss of a gear in a less painful way. Often
the control lever can't get the hub into the low or

middle gear at all. To get the gears working, you have to get some oil into the hub, then adjust the little indicator chain that goes into it.

To oil a three-speed hub, find the lubricating nipple, which sticks up out of the smooth cylindrical section, in between the spokes. Get a can of *light*, high-grade oil, like the pink 10 weight Automatic Transmission Fluid (ATF) they use in cars, or good bicycle gear oil. Open the little cap on the lubricating nipple, using your fingernail carefully so you don't break it or tear the cover off. Then stick the end of your oil can into the hole and squirt about three or four healthy slugs of the stuff in there. You may have to do it slowly to prevent overflow. Close the nipple cover and put a couple of drops of oil on the indicator where it enters the hub.

To adjust the three-speed hub, put the control lever into its middle position (often marked "2" or "N"), then loosen (cl) the little knurled locknut on the indicator (see illustration 30). Then turn the adjusting sleeve up and down until you can look into the hole in the big axle nut and see the end of the smooth pole of the indicator just barely sticking out of the end of the axle. On some models of three-speed, you will see an arrow or an "N" appearing in a little hole in the big axle nut. Center the mark in the hole on these types of bikes. When your middle gear is adjusted, lock the locknut up (c-cl) against the adjusting sleeve firmly, so the thing won't come loose again.

If you still get slippage, make sure the metal band that holds the cable ferrule (see illustration 30) is cinched tight (cl) by its mounting bolt. If that still

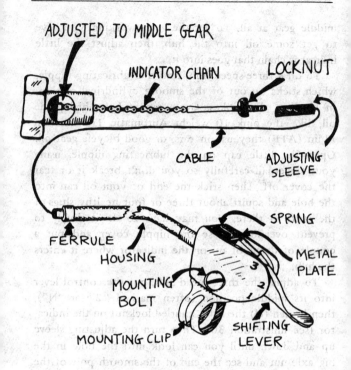

Illustration #30
THREE SPEED CONTROL

doesn't stop the slippage, your hub or cable or indicator chain must be messed up. Ride the bike home in high gear (with the cable loosened, so it *can't* slip loose on you), and replace the cable and indicator, and, if needed, take the wheel to a top-notch shop for a complete hub overhaul.

Derailleur Type Changers

If you have *gear slippage*, particularly a tendency of the chain to slip from a large sprocket to a smaller one, either front or rear, the control lever is probably loose. See Control Lever PROBLEMS.

If your *chain is throwing*, find out if it throws off a front one or a rear one, then see Front Changer PROBLEMS or Rear Changer PROBLEMS. Two hints can save you from many chain throwing problems: *Don't ever lay your ten-speed down on its tender right side! Don't ever backpedal while shifting a ten-speed!*

If your *chain rubs or makes grindy noises* as you pedal, first fiddle a bit with the lever for the front changer, and see if the chain is rubbing the side-plates of the front changer. If it is, and your lever-adjustment doesn't move the cage clear of the chain, see *rubbing* on page 115. If grindy noises persist after that, and your chain is oiled, the problem may be that a sprocket is bent. See Sprocket PROBLEMS.

If all of those things are OK and you still have grindy noises, you may simply be using a combination of sprockets that your bike isn't up to using. On some ten-speed bikes, it isn't possible for the chain to run from the biggest front sprocket to the biggest rear one, or from the smallest front one to the smallest rear sprocket. The chain runs at too sharp an angle; it is either stretched too tight or sagging too loose. It's a strain on the whole system, and it lets you know by grinding and rubbing.

If this is the case with your bike, avoid using those very extreme sprocket combinations; the gears can be matched with other combinations of sprockets, anyway.

Control Lever or Tip Shifter

PROBLEMS: *Slippage or stickies.* Either your lever is really easy to move, and shifts by itself when you let it go, or it's so hard to move you can't shift smoothly. Do not oil the lever! Usually, the problem with a slipping or sticky control lever is simply the adjustment of the wing screw or (on a handlebar tip shifter) the pivot bolt.

On a regular control lever, just tighten (cl) or loosen (c-cl) the wing screw until the lever shifts smoothly, but stays put after you've shifted it.

To adjust a tip shifter, you have to loosen (c-cl) the slotted locknut on the end of the pivot bolt. This may be hard to do with the little screwdriver in your road kit; put it in the slot on one side and turn firmly. Adjust the pivot bolt when you have the locknut loose (cl tightens, c-cl loosens) and make sure to leave a little looseness so the thing will shift easily. The ratchet gismo in the lever will hold it in position on a gear unless the pivot bolt is really loose. If the ratchet breaks, it is very hard to get the pivot bolt adjusted in such a way that it'll hold the lever in a gear and still allow shifting. If you're stuck out in the boonies with this problem, just put the lever in the middle gear position (or low gear, for a front changer), then tighten (cl) the pivot bolt until the gears won't change. You can ride home using the other changer, then take the shifter apart and replace the tiny ratchet parts, or just replace the whole unit.

If you get gear slippage even when you're sure your lever is OK, the problem is most likely a loose cable anchor bolt. Go on to Cable PROBLEMS.

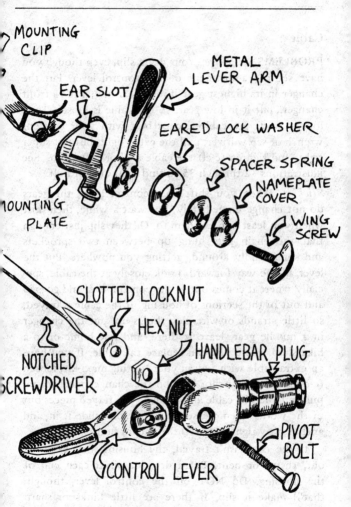

Illustration #31
TEN SPEED CONTROL LEVERS

Cable

PROBLEMS: *Slippage.* Your gears slip, even though you have set the adjustment of the control lever. Put the changer in its highest gear if it's a rear one; if it's a front changer, put it in low gear, so the cable is loose. Then loosen (c-cl) the cable anchor bolt with your crescent wrench or screwdriver, pull the cable tight, but not super tight, and tighten (c-cl) the cable anchor bolt again. See illustrations 32 through 35 to find your anchor bolt.

Stickies. When you shift your control lever, the gears do not change immediately, but wait a while, then shift when you least expect them to. Or they slip just enough that the chain gets hung up between two sprockets and spins wildly around, getting you nowhere. Put the lever all the way forward. Look closely at the cable, specially where it comes out of the control lever and goes in and out of the sections of housing. If the cable is frayed, so little strands of wire clog things up, put the changer in a middle gear, leave it there, and ride home or to a bike shop where you can replace the cable. If you have an extra cable with you in your touring maxi-kit, loosen (c-cl) the cable anchor bolt on the changer mechanism, pull out the old cable and clean all the frayed pieces out of the works, then grease the new cable, slide it in, and anchor it by tightening (cl) the anchor bolt.

If the cable isn't frayed, the housing may be dried out, rusty, or bent. Put a drop of oil at each end of the housing. Do NOT oil the control lever, though; that'll make it slip. If there are little kinks or sharp bends in the housing (these often appear near the ends of the short piece of housing that is next to the rear changer mechanism) hold the housing on both sides of the bend firmly with your fingers and straighten it.

If none of these remedies help your gear stickies, the problem is probably a stiff changer mechanism. See Front Changer PROBLEMS or Rear Changer PROBLEMS.

Front Changer

PROBLEMS: *Rubbing.* The cage of the front changer rubs against one side or the other of the chain and makes a bothersome noise. First try to eliminate the noise with the control lever. Shifting the rear changer often necessitates adjustment of the front one. Make sure the adjustable bolt on the control lever is tight enough (see Control Lever PROBLEMS).

Still got rubbing? Get the bike up on a fence post, or get a friend to hold the rear wheel up, and put your head above the front changer. Crank the pedals forward slowly (if you can't find anything to hang the bike up on, pedal them backwards) and watch the chain where it passes between the sides of the front changer cage. You may see a wobble in your sprocket every time it goes around. If so, go to Front Sprocket PROBLEMS. If the chain hits because it is running at a very sharp angle from the front to rear sprockets, you've an extreme gear position that won't work (see page 111).

The next thing to check out is the alignment of the changer. Are the sides of the cage parallel with the front sprockets? Are the sides of the cage straight and vertical?

If the whole cage isn't parallel with the front sprockets, loosen (c-cl) the bolt or bolts that cinch the changer around the bike frame. Don't take the bolts all the way

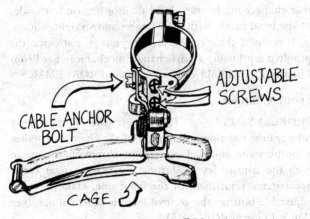

Illustration #32
FRONT CHANGER

out — just loosen them a bit. Slide the changer up or down the seat tube until it is at such a level that the outer side plate of the cage is lined up about ¼ inch above the ends of the teeth on the large sprocket. Then twist it to the right and left until that same outer side plate is exactly parallel with the sprocket when you look down on it from above. Don't let the angle of the chain fool you; focus on the line of the outer side plate and the line of the sprocket, and get them parallel. Tighten (cl) the bolt or bolts that hold the changer to the bike frame and check the alignment from the side and above again. Sometimes tightening those bolts will take the changer out of alignment. If it does, loosen them and try again, until the changer is properly aligned.

If the sides of the cage are bent or twisted out of the

vertical plane, get out your crescent wrench and adjust the jaws so they just slip onto the bent side plate. Bend the plate with care and patience, until it is as near to straight, vertical, and aligned as you can get it. You may have to loosen (c-cl) the bolt that holds the changer to the bike frame yet again, to re-align the thing.

If your straightened and aligned cage still rubs, you have to adjust how far it moves when you move the control lever. That's pretty easy on bikes that have front changers like the one in illustration 32, with two adjustable screws. Just put the bike in its lowest gear (small front sprocket, biggest rear sprocket). Figure out which adjustable screw controls the inward range of the cage (one of the screw tips will be closer to hitting the changer body), and adjust the screw so that innermost side of the cage barely clears the chain when you turn the cranks around. Then put the bike in the highest possible gear (big front sprocket, smallest rear one) and adjust the other screw so the outer side of the cage barely clears the flowing chain.

If you have one of those odd-ball front changers with only one adjustable bolt, do the same procedure, but move the whole cage on its push-rod to get it clear of the chain in the lowest gear (loosen and tighten the little bolt that holds it on the rod). Use the single adjustable screw to limit the range of the cage in the high gear position.

OK, so you've got the range adjusted for your front changer. Try shifting the bike through the gears as you ride around in a circle. Chain no longer rubbing? Good. Chain throwing now? Bad. Go on to the next section.

Chain throwing, or changer won't shift chain. When you shift the front changer, it either throws the chain right off the sprockets, or it won't move the chain enough to get it on the other sprocket, or it puts the chain out where you tangle your pedals up in it and grind to a halt. Most unpleasant.

First check the alignment and adjustment of the changer, as in the *Rubbing* section just above, and make sure that when the changers are in the highest and lowest gear positions, the sides of the front changer are *barely* missing the cage. If the cage isn't parallel to the sprockets, or if it can move in or out too far, it will throw the chain for sure.

If your problem is a chain that always throws off the big sprocket when you try to shift to it, and no amount of adjusting stops the problem, slip your crescent wrench jaws onto the front tip of the outer side plate of the cage, and bend it in very slightly, about 1/16 of an inch or so. This slightly bent-in cage tip will catch a chain that has throwing tendencies.

If your adjusted front changer can't get the chain *onto* one of the sprockets, the cable may be either too tight or too loose. Loosen (c-cl) the anchor bolt that holds the end of it and tighten or loosen the cable, as needed. Then tighten (cl) the anchor bolt and check the function of the gear changer to make sure it's still adjusted right.

If your front changer is all adjusted, aligned, and spiffy, but your chain *still* throws off all the time, not just when you're shifting, but when you go over bumps in turns and things, you might have a very old, flobby chain. See Chain PROBLEMS. If the chain is in good shape, the problem might be that the whole power train is out of alignment. Ride to a good shop to have that checked out by a pro. It really requires the eye and tools of an expert to diagnose and correct.

Rear Changer

PROBLEMS: *Chain throwing* off, or not making it onto either the biggest or smallest rear sprocket. Your changer needs to be aligned and adjusted at *both* the high and low ends of its range. Make sure your chain is clean and oiled before you start this whole procedure.

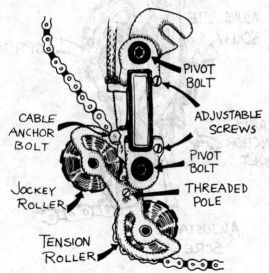

Illustration #33
SOLID BODY CHANGER (DERAILLEUR)

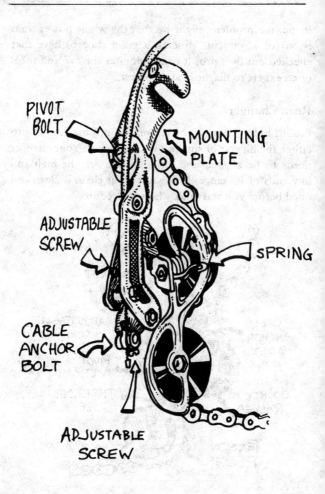

PIVOT BOLT

MOUNTING PLATE

ADJUSTABLE SCREW

SPRING

CABLE ANCHOR BOLT

ADJUSTABLE SCREW

Illustration #34
SPINDLY-ARMED CHANGER (DERAILLEUR)

Start with the alignment and adjustment of the high end of the gear range. Put the bike up on a fence pole or in the hands of your willing friend, so the rear wheel is off the ground, then push the control lever for the rear changer all the way forward as you pedal the cranks around. If the chain throws off the small sprocket, pull the control lever back a bit until the chain will feed onto the smallest sprocket smoothly. If the chain can't make it onto that smallest sprocket because the cable is too tight, loosen (c-cl) the cable anchor bolt, then loosen up the cable and tighten (cl) the anchor bolt again.

Now turn the adjustable screw in or out slowly until you feel that the tip of it is in light contact with the nub or metal side of the changer body. Turn the pedals and see that the chain is feeding smoothly onto the smallest sprocket. If you can't even find the adjustable range screw, look at illustrations 33 through 35. You may have one of those nice changers on which they marked the screws; in that case, look for the one with the "H" next to it.

When you've found the right screw and turned it in and out gently a few times, and adjusted it until you feel the tip of it just touch the thing on the changer, back the screw off (c-cl) a quarter turn. This will give the changer a bit of play, so it can shift into the gear easily.

OK, your changer is now feeding the chain onto the smallest sprocket. Check the alignment to make sure the chain will feed onto the sprocket *smoothly*. Get a straight stick or piece of metal, or set the bike straight up and down with a telephone pole behind it. Eyeball your straight stick or an edge of the phone pole in the background so it lines up with the roller cage of the gear changer, as in illustration 36.

When you eyeball the line of the rollers from straight behind the bike, it should be parallel to the lines made by the sprockets, which you're seeing on edge. If the roller cage is pointing either in toward the wheel or out at the air, you have to try to straighten it. This is hard to do without fancy tools. If you have an allen key that fits the hex-shaped holes in the pivot bolts of your changer, stick the long end of the key in the upper pivot bolt, the one nearest to the drop-out where the wheel axle is held. Now push up or down on the key and

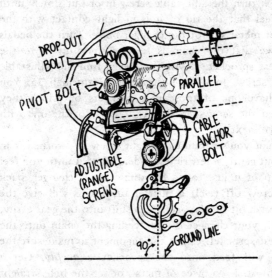

Illustration #35
SLANT PANTOGRAPH CHANGER

see if you can bend the changer mounting plate so it holds the roller cage parallel to the rear sprockets. The key may bend first. In that case, you have to ride home with the bent changer and fix it there with tools that don't mess it up.

If you can get the changer straight, test the thing to make sure it still can get the chain on and off the smallest sprocket. Adjust the adjustable screw if it needs it.

To set the changer's low gear range adjustment, first make sure the high range is OK, as above, then shift the bike into its lowest gear. What's that? The chain goes into the spokes? Tough luck. If it's jammed in

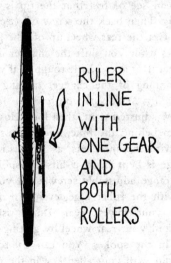

RULER
IN LINE
WITH
ONE GEAR
AND
BOTH
ROLLERS

Illustration #36
REAR CHANGER ALIGNMENT

there, hold the wheel still from behind the bike and pull the chain up out of where it's stuck, starting at the front of the sprocket and working back around it. Yuch! When you've got the chain free, fiddle with the control lever until the chain feeds onto the largest sprocket. If the changer can't quite get the chain onto that sprocket, you have to loosen (c-cl) the low range adjustable screw and maybe tighten the cable until the changer will move far enough to get the chain onto the largest sprocket.

When the chain is flowing onto the biggest sprocket smoothly, tighten (cl) the low range adjustable screw until you can see or feel that the tip is nudging against something. Then back the screw off (c-cl) about a quarter turn. Get the rear wheel up off the ground and turn the cranks while you shift the changer in and out of its lowest gear. If it goes a little rough or if you hear a plunk plunk-plunking of the changer tapping on the spokes, *stop pedaling.* Make sure you have the low range adjustable screw adjusted right, then look closely at the roller cage from behind the bike, and make sure the thing is parallel with the sprockets, as in illustration 36. If the roller cage is bent in so it hits the spokes, tighten (cl) the low range adjustable screw until you *can't* hit the spokes with the roller cage, even if it means you can't get into your lowest gear. Don't risk ruining your changer and your rear wheel by getting that roller cage jammed in the spokes. You can try to straighten the changer out with your allen key in the upper pivot bolt hole, as described in the high range alignment above, but if you can't get it straight, just ride home or to a good shop with only four gears in the back.

If the changer is lined up and the adjustable screw is set right, but the chain still falters a lot trying to get up onto the biggest sprocket, you may have one of the following problems, listed in the order of probability: a sticky changer, an old, loose, or squeaky chain, a sticky cable, or a power train that's out of alignment. All but the last problem can be solved by looking them up in this book. If the whole power train is out of alignment, you have to live with it or go to a real pro bike mechanic to get things straight.

Sticky changer. The changer or derailleur is sluggish in shifting the chain from one sprocket to another, especially onto the smallest and largest sprockets, and you have checked the control lever and cable for stickiness. First off, try a little oil at the joints of the changer body. On some old-style changers, the joints are held together with bolts and nuts. These can be loosened just a hair, oiled, and re-set so they pivot a tiny bit looser.

If the changer is bent or old and beat up, it'll be best to replace it at the next good bike shop you get to. In most cases this requires only loosening (c-cl) the cable anchor bolt, the mounting plate bolt (or, on fancy bikes, the upper pivot bolt), and the bolt that holds the tension roller to the roller cage. Pull the cable out, take the jockey roller off and remove the chain, then take the whole changer off. Do the reverse to get the new changer on, making sure you have the chain flowing in that reverse "S" shape through the rollers. Adjust the adjustable screws carefully on your new changer, so its range is correct, and you're ready to ride again.

Chain loose, or feeding roughly. Either your chain sags when the rear changer is in high gear, or your changer does not take up the slack in the low front gear position, or you often hear grindy noises down there. First check the chain age and length (see Chain PROBLEMS). Next, take a good look at the changer, especially the chain rollers and their cage. Are the rollers covered with gunk? Is the pivot of the cage all gunked up? Clean the rollers and cage with solvent if they need it. Oil the rollers, too. If the changer is bent or broken as well as dirty, you have to limp to a bike shop and replace the thing.

If there is a spring that is out in the open, as on the changer shown in illustration 34, take a pair of pliers and move the end of the spring to a hook that makes it tighter if you can. On most changers, however, the spring is harder to get at. You'd be best off riding home with your loose chain and tackling the spring tightening or replacement, where you've got better tools and a clean place to put all the little parts you have to dismantle.

Postscript

This isn't the end. On my next bike ride, I bet I have some problem I haven't covered in this book. Or, more likely, *you'll* have a hassle on *your* next ride, and find that I didn't cover it well enough. If you do, write to me, c/o the publisher, so the book can be improved in the future. Just as there will always be another road to ride down, there will always be another bike problem to tinker with and overcome. Keep tinkering, and keep riding!

ANYBODY'S BIKE BOOK
New Revised and Expanded Edition
by Tom Cuthbertson, illustrated by Rick Morrall
Classic manual for owners and buyers of one-speed,
three-speed, and ten-speed bikes. Immensely readable
and clearly illustrated. Guides the do-it-yourselfer
in finding the problem and fixing it fast.
6 x 9 inches, 192 pages, $4.95 paper, $8.95 cloth

BETTER BIKES!
A Manual for an Alternative Mode of Transportation
by Tom Cuthbertson, illustrated by Karen Lusebrink
"Bikes are perfect examples of E. F. Shumacher's
principles: they are small, beautiful machines, built
to human proportions, made for efficiency, and made
to last. Bikes are not as fast as cars, and cannot go
as far, but this book can help people find out just
how much they *can* do, and how much fun they can
be along the way." There are millions of bicycles
in garages awaiting a strategy to put them back to
work and this book does it.
6 x 9 inches, 128 pages, $4.95 paper, $7.95 cloth

ANYBODY'S ROLLER SKATING BOOK
by Tom Cuthbertson, illustrated by Rick Morrall
and Karen Lusebrink. Photographs by Franklin Avery
First full size edition of Tom's successful book about
rollerskating. Covers basics (Getting Started on Rental
Skates, Skating Forward and Backward, History of
Roller Skates) to what you need to know when getting
your own skates (Buyer's Guide; Adjustments & Repairs).
6 x 9 inches, 208 pages, $4.95 paper, $8.95 cloth

Available at your local bookstore, or order direct pre-paid
from TEN SPEED PRESS, Box 7123, Berkeley, CA 94707.
Please include $.50 additional for each paperback, or $.75
additional for each clothbound copy for postage & handling.

Appendix

CATALOGUES FOR TOOLS AND PARTS

BIG WHEEL LTD.
340 Holly Street
Denver, CO 80220

BIKECOLOGY
Catalogue Department
P.O. Box 1880
Santa Monica, CA 90406

CYCLOPEDIA
311 North Mitchell Street
Cadillac, MI 49601

SINK'S BICYCLE WORLD
816 S. Washington Street
Marion, IN 46952

TOURING CYCLIST SHOP
P.O. Box 378
Boulder, CO 80302

WHEEL GOODS CORP.
2737 Hennepin Avenue
Minneapolis, MN 55408

REPAIR MANUALS

Anybody's Bike Book, New Revised Edition,
  Tom Cuthbertson, Ten Speed Press, 1979

Richard's Bicycle Book, R. Ballantine, Ballantine, 1976

Glenn's Complete Bicycle Manual, Glenn and Coles,
  Crown, 1973

Building Bicycle Wheels, Robert Wright, World, 1976

TOURING ORGANIZATIONS

American Youth Hostels (AYH), Delaplane, VA 22025

International Bicycle Touring Society,
  846 Prospect Street, La Jolla, CA 92037

Bikecentennial Routing Service,
  P.O. Box 8308-A, Missoula, MT 59807

BIKE SHOPS ON MY ROUTE

Name

Address

Phone

Name

Address

Phone

Name

Address

Phone

Name

Address

Phone

Name

Address

Phone

BIKE SHOPS ON MY ROUTE

Name _____

Address _____

Phone _____

Name _____

Address _____

Phone _____

Name _____

Address _____

Phone _____

Name _____

Address _____

Phone _____

Name _____

Address _____

Phone _____

BIKE SHOPS ON MY ROUTE

Name

Address

Phone

Name

Address

Phone

Name

Address

Phone

Name

Address

Phone

Name

Address

Phone